WITCHCRAFT
FOR
BEGINNERS

Empowering the Modern Witch with an Easy-to-Follow Guide to Spellcasting, Wicca Rituals, and Protection Magick

❧ Eleanor Clemm ☙

© Copyright 2022 - All rights reserved.

The content contained within this book may not be reproduced, duplicated or transmitted without direct written permission from the author or the publisher.

Under no circumstances will any blame or legal responsibility be held against the publisher, or author, for any damages, reparation, or monetary loss due to the information contained within this book, either directly or indirectly.

Legal Notice:

This book is copyright protected. It is only for personal use. You cannot amend, distribute, sell, use, quote or paraphrase any part, or the content within this book, without the consent of the author or publisher.

Disclaimer Notice:

Please note the information contained within this document is for educational and entertainment purposes only. All effort has been executed to present accurate, up to date, reliable, complete information. No warranties of any kind are declared or implied. Readers acknowledge that the author is not engaged in the rendering of legal, financial, medical or professional advice. The content within this book has been derived from various sources. Please consult a licensed professional before attempting any techniques outlined in this book.

By reading this document, the reader agrees that under no circumstances is the author responsible for any losses, direct or indirect, that are incurred as a result of the use of the information contained within this document, including, but not limited to, errors, omissions, or inaccuracies.

Dedicated to my wonderful mother,
who has always believed in and supported me.

Thank you for showing me that
there is infinite magick in the world.

Table of Contents

	INTRODUCTION	1
CHAPTER 1	TAPPING INTO YOUR POWER	8
CHAPTER 2	MODERN WITCHCRAFT	39
CHAPTER 3	THE WITCH'S TOOL KIT	59
CHAPTER 4	RUNES AND SYMBOLS	76
CHAPTER 5	SPELLCASTING AND RITUALS	106
CHAPTER 6	BANISHING, MANIFESTING, PROTECTING	150
CHAPTER 7	WHAT THE UNIVERSE CAN TELL YOU	163
	CONCLUSION	190
	REFERENCES	194

Your Free Gift

As a way of saying thank you for your purchase, I am offering the book 50 POWERFUL SPELL JAR RECIPES *FREE* to my readers.

Get instant access by scanning the QR Code below with your phone.

INSIDE THIS BOOK YOU WILL DISCOVER:

- How to prepare your jars for maximum potency
- Everything you need to make your spell jars effective
- 50 different spell jar recipes sorted by category

Add 50 spells to your library today
by downloading your free book now
at fireboltbooks.com

Witchcraft for Beginners

Empowering the Modern Witch with an Easy-to-Follow Guide to Spellcasting, Wicca Rituals, and Protection Magick

INTRODUCTION

Whether or not we have the courage to admit it to ourselves, there will always be times where we are unsure in which direction life is going. Times where we're confused and perhaps even frustrated that we don't know which path to take and have fears that the decisions we make will cause us to fall into a proverbial canyon that we won't be able to climb out of. You are not alone, everyone in the world feels this way at one time or another.

If this is how you have been feeling for a long time or even if you just feel like you need some additional fulfillment or just need a helping hand with a difficult decision, then I am here to help you through these times. I have had my share of struggles throughout life and magick has always been there to help guide me throughout my troubled times.

I have been practicing witchcraft since I was in my late teens, but I have been around magick my entire life; having been surrounded by it and been partially taught by the person that I admire the most: my mother, and the rest of my path having been filled by my own independent researching and experimenting. Learning and growing has not only healed any pain that I had encountered throughout my life, but has also kept me on a path of happiness and contentment in addition to filling me with confidence about not just my decisions, but my life in general.

And yet I still felt like there was something missing that I couldn't put my finger on and it was only after careful consideration and examination of myself did I realize what it was: the knowledge that I had, and still am, accumulating is only benefitting myself, but hasn't been benefiting others. That is the motivation behind writing this book, to give advice to people that weren't as lucky as me to have a mentor to guide them along like I had my mom.

But I'm not just going to give you instructions on how to find your path to fulfillment, this isn't a manual, or a textbook, I'm not here to just give you facts and throw you in the ocean with just a life preserver. No, I am here as a guide to help you find your own way to personal happiness and fulfillment with genuine advice and guidance.

Again, I'm not here to just give information just for the sake of giving it out, I want to show you that anyone can learn magick at any time of their life. While admittedly, this book is mostly aimed at beginners/newcomers/baby witches, anyone can benefit from this book. I want to demonstrate how anyone can start out small with all aspects of witchcraft, whether it would be your abilities or even your tool kit; all that's needed is the right kind of belief, focus, mindset, patience and practice.

I don't doubt that you are eager to dive into reading the rest of this book right away, however, before we truly begin our journey, I would first like to go over the history of witchcraft to whet your appetite. But before we do that, I would like to clear up a common source of confusion, and that is the interchangeable use of the words 'Wiccan,' 'witch,' and 'pagan.'

A Wiccan refers to a person who is following the Wiccan/spiritual path and has either followed through with a Wiccan initiation or has formally and ritually declared themselves as Wiccan.

Now some Wiccans do use the words 'Wiccan' and 'witch' interchangeably, but some people who consider themselves witches don't consider themselves Wiccan. In fact, Wiccans are in actuality a subgroup of witches.

In addition, Wiccans and witches are both subgroups of pagans. By definition, pagans are people who practice earth based religions. Many Wiccans and witches think of themselves being pagan but not all pagans see themselves as Wiccans and witches.

For more clarity about this book, when I use the word "witchcraft" I am referring to what Wiccans and witches do, which is rituals and spell casting.

Now for the history lesson, Wicca itself is both a "new and old" religion as well as an evolving one that combines folk traditions that have survived the ages, modern elements and what is made up by individual practitioners for suitability or purpose for a situation that they feel requires their own touch.

Some of the Wicca's structure comes from Western European pagan rituals that had been practiced for centuries, like a celebration of a harvest, looking over the cycle of seasons and even just a worship of nature. However, most of the practices are more modern and can be gleaned from medieval era magick books and organizations like the Golden Dawn.

We should also address the very large elephant in the room in regards to practicing witchcraft: the negative stereotypes that had begun with the persecution of pagans by the Christian church and are still in effect today, such as those hideous Halloween decorations. The kinds of people that they had deemed to be 'witches' that were 'evil' were the healers and shamans and wise people of their communities who were respected and appreciated for the skills that they used for the community's benefit.

Not that there aren't people with the skills and talents who use them for more destructive purposes, if the potential is there and they are willing to ignore the rules of decency then they will do so, as we will cover in chapter 6.

Witchcraft stems from understanding that we are all interconnected, whether it is with each other or the earth itself. And yet, that does not mean that there were never any primary deities that are worshiped; in Wicca, there are deities that are referred to as the God and the Goddess.

The God, who is called the Lord in some traditions, is said to be connected to the sun as its ruler and is known as the Horned God of the forest who watches over wild animals and our hunting activities. Deities who represent the God in his horned form include the Celtic god Cernunnos and the Greek god Pan. From the connection of the sun, this part of him projects the energy of all life and is responsible for the formation of the Wiccan calendar due to his yearlong trip around the Earth; many of the ancient deities that are connected to the sun include the Egyptian god Ra and the Greek god Apollo.

In addition, he possesses masculine energy as well as procreation and so is connected to sex and is represented by phallic symbols such as the previously mentioned horns, but also arrows, spears, swords and wands.

As for his counterpart, the Goddess, she possesses the receptive energy to his projective, she is the Earth that gives life, and this influence includes the oceans and the moon. She is a nurturer who has been also referred to as the Lady in some traditions and as the Great Mother in others, she also associates with domesticated animals.

The Goddess is actually represented by three aspects of herself, each aspect is connected to the stages of a woman's reproductive life: Maiden, Mother, and Crone as well as to three of the moon phases: waxing, full, and waning; some ancient societies have portrayed her as having three faces with each one being connected to an aspect. Some Wiccans refer to her as the Triple Moon Goddess, or more simply, the Triple Goddess.

Regardless of how she is named by her followers, every aspect of her has a role in the Earth's life cycles and of those who inhabit it. Symbols that are connected to her receptive energy include cauldrons and cups, they also include her gifts like fruits and flowers. She is also represented by the Egyptian goddess Isis and the Celtic Brigid with further goddesses representing each of her aspects such as the Greek Artemis for the Maiden, the Roman Ceres for the Mother, and the Greek Hecate for the Crone.

But just knowing the history is not enough to get one started on the path of magickal practice, you also need to figure out who you are, or more accurately, what kind of magickal practitioner you are aligned with. We will go through all of that in the next chapter before we truly dive into the magick of this book.

However, there is one last thing of note before we move on, and it is to say that there actually aren't a lot of rules on how we, or any other witchcraft practitioner, can use our craft. That being said, the few basic rules that do exist warn us against using our magick for selfish and/or harmful purposes, whether it is the threefold law or the "Wiccan's Rede," which will be touched on in chapter two.

But do not be concerned about bringing positivity to ourselves being considered a selfish act, as it is not about bringing things to ourselves at the expense of others. In actuality, it is rather about finding peace and bringing what we are missing to ourselves, whether it is love, prosperity, good health, or protection. This book is here to help you find those missing pieces of yourself so that you can create and take ownership of your own destiny.

Now let us begin.

Chapter 1

TAPPING INTO YOUR POWER

I understand if you are feeling a little eager to jump into practicing magick right away, and you want to try it right now! But you need to take a deep breath and slow down my friend. Diving into the deep ocean before learning to swim may be detrimental. Similarly practicing magick without understanding the basics isn't recommended!

That is the goal of this book; however, the first three chapters will be about the bare basics, such as the usage of magick in everyday life and what tools you might want or need. Most witches have at least some natural abilities. If you are able to harness your natural abilities, you will begin to tap into your true power. Let's discuss the different types of witches and find the one that speaks to you most.

You might be surprised to know that there is a vast number of types of witches out there. You may have already heard of a few of them like a "kitchen witch," or a "green witch," but there are many more paths available to us. It is important for you to not just understand the differences between each one, but to appreciate their uniqueness. Here are twenty of the common types of witches along with some key points that you might identify yourself with.

Types of Witches

Art Witch

Art witches focus on creative expression; it is an important part of their spiritual practice, whether it is crafting, painting, sewing, writing or any other kind of creative endeavor as creating beauty around them helps to connect them to the divine and spirituality. Decorating their book of shadows and setting up altars to their particular tastes are deeply fulfilling to them. However, they are challenged by needing to find ways of expressing their creativity without feeling judged, whether it is by others, or by themselves.

Astro Witch

Astro witches' primary form of practice lies in astrology; it is important to them that they study the heavens and the movements of the celestial bodies and they are eager to explore the way people and the world are influenced by their energy. They do face challenges in that they have difficulty not allowing the heavens to tell them what to do, and they can get nervous and possibly feel doubt about their actions rather than feel empowered.

CEREMONIAL WITCH

The Ceremonial witches have many practices; however, they hold the highest regard for ceremonial and ritual practices they work with the most and will likely work one of them into whatever it is they are trying to accomplish, whether it is casting a spell or otherwise. They will also often call to specific beings and entities to aid them in their spellcasting.

COSMIC WITCH

Cosmic witches, who are also called 'star' witches, are a little different than the majority of the witch types out there, rather than rely on the magick that exists on our planet, they look to the magick that exists in the cosmos; such as astrology and even astronomy, as well as celestial energy. These are witches who base their spells and rituals upon following the alignments of the stars and planets and their different placements.

ECLECTIC WITCH

Eclectic witches don't have just a single set of practice, culture, tradition or religion that they use, rather their practice comes from many sources and basically becomes the witches' own. They may worship a higher being, be mainly secular, or even have their own kind of spirituality; they ultimately make their own 'rules' and it is entirely unique to each of the individual witches.

ELEMENTAL WITCH

Elemental magick is based around honoring each of the elements; an elemental witch may choose to have an altar for each element. The elements are what they call upon for their spells and rituals and there might even be one element that they personally connect with and put more effort toward finding. When we talk about the elements that elemental witches connect with, it refers to earth, air, fire, and water, but we may also say that wind is a separate element as well. In addition, the element of water has its own separate way of being worshiped by sea witches who are discussed later.

EMPATH WITCH

Empath witches focus mainly on their emotions and intuitions, they can easily pick up on the energies, moods, and vibes of those around them. Their unique powers can be helpful in healing others as well as feel fulfilled from practicing meditation and divination. But they can be challenged by having difficulty in finding balance between helping others and themselves; they need to learn to set up boundaries and protect themselves from others' negativity.

GREEN WITCH

Green witches, who are also called "garden" or "forest" witches, are well connected to the earth and the energy that it possesses. Green witches may have their own home gardens where they grow their own herbs for their spells. They also spend time getting in touch with nature in their home area and practice with the local plants and environment. They also use any combination of greenery and plants in their magick, their cooking, or inside their homes.

HEDGE WITCH

Hedge witches practice something called "hedge jumping," which is basically leaving "this world" for what they call the "Otherworld," which is also known as the spiritual world, and also has the ability to send messages between both worlds. Hedge witches practice astral projection in addition to working with Earth based magick. What makes them different from other witches is their ability to cross the "hedge," which refers to the boundary between this world and the spirit world.

HEREDITARY WITCH

Hereditary witches are born into witchcraft, it is a part of their family and perhaps even their lineage. These are the witches whose craft is passed down from previous generations. They may choose to work with their own individual practices instead of their families'.

KITCHEN WITCH

Kitchen witches, also known as "home" or "hearth" witches, create most of their magick in their homes or in their kitchens as their name implies. The home of a kitchen witch is a very special, sacred place. They gain enjoyment from brewing, cooking, and using herbs, sometimes ones that have been picked from their own garden. Their practice combines their own magickal energy with everyday objects, as well as food, herbs, and essential oils to create their magick, their rituals, and their spells.

LUNAR WITCH

Lunar witches are deeply connected to the cycles of the moon, more so than other witches. They hold rituals during any phase of the moon and have a desire to understand how the moon affects them emotionally and physically, and doing so allows them to be in tune with their own natural cycles and rhythms.

SEA WITCH

As the name might infer, sea witches have strong bonds to the element of water and use it the most often in their practice, not just an attachment to seas or oceans. Sea witches practice the kinds of magick that use objects that one can find with bodies of water, such as shells, sand, and even driftwood. They also have a strong connection with ancient lore that involves water and its beings such as sirens and mermaids.

SECULAR WITCH

Secular witches are practitioners who still use tools like crystals, candles, herbs etc. but don't attach any kind of spirituality to their practice. They don't worship a deity or any kind of higher being, they are non-religious. They also don't believe that there is power behind energy or that there is energy in their practice. However, that doesn't mean that secular witches can't be spiritual, it just means that their practice isn't spiritual as they would consider it two separate things.

SHADOW WITCH

Shadow witches are magick practitioners whose focus is on what is called "shadow work." Shadow work is a form of learning to be aware of yourself, as well as to understand and transform their "shadows" which hold them back into aspects that make them stronger by delving deep into themselves. But the path isn't all gloomy, the transformation involved is a path of bright light.

SOLAR WITCH

While the moon gets almost all the attention in the witchcraft community, solar witches just love to soak up the energy of the sun; just being outside on a sunny day is an important part of their practice, and they might even enjoy performing rituals during those days. Being a solar witch means that the Sabbats are an important part of their practice as they are based around the sun's movements, especially the summer solstice. However, they may have a little bit of trouble connecting with the rest of the witchcraft community because of their primary interest in the sun over the moon.

SOLITARY WITCH

Solitary witches aren't a separate type of witch, they can fit along with any other type of practitioner, but what makes them solitary is that they work alone rather than in a group. This could either be by personal choice or because they haven't found a group yet.

TRADITIONAL WITCH

Traditional witchcraft places a lot of focus on the historical practices of magick and is based on the "Old Craft" that predates Wicca. Often these witches study their ancestors' practices or other old lore that is attached to witchcraft. Traditional witches want to honor these "old ways" of the craft and tend to focus on the local history and spirits of where they are or where they came from. While they hold old history and customs in high regard, there are traditional witches that are considered contemporary who practice today.

WARRIOR WITCH

Warrior witches are fierce people who choose to express it through witchcraft, they are deeply connected to the element of fire and it shows in how they have a need to take action and protect loved ones and even strangers. They have a strong sense of right and wrong in their own belief systems and will fight for what they believe in, such as activism, protesting, or defending ideas and people they care about. Warrior witches have a strong connection with protection spells and may feel close to warrior deities like Athena.

WILD WITCH

Wild witches are very much connected with nature's wilderness; they differ from that of a garden witch in that their interest lies in the wild and not the tamed gardens that the latter enjoys. Wild witches are those who love long hikes in the forest and prefer to be the only human for miles as well as creating temporary altars among the wilderness. Wild witches do face challenges in how they can connect with the wilds in their daily lives, given how difficult it can be these days.

These twenty examples are only a starting point in finding your magickal path; they are meant to help give you an overview of the variety you can discover.

SO, WHO ARE YOU?

So how does one determine what type of witch they are? Even after reading over the types mentioned above, you still might be feeling a little lost and that's perfectly okay, I was a little lost too when I first started out despite my mom's guidance. But that is what I'm here for, to help you find your way along your path and to help you find out who you are as a witch.

So, where do you really begin your search? If you were to type in Google something along the lines of "how to discover your witch type" or a similar phrase, chances are that a lot of the results that do pop up are quizzes and that's not a problem per se, it is just that quizzes aren't really the best way to go because they are varied in their questions and results and there is a limit on the results as well. Out of curiosity I took a few of these quizzes and my results were quite varied and not even close to who I really am.

But if quizzes are out, then what's in? Well one thing that can help is reading, but not the kind of article reading that I touched on above, rather you should only focus on topics that interest you, but you also need to be careful not to overwhelm yourself with too much information. Rather let your own intuition guide you to the research that supports you instead of overwhelming you. Read about different witchcraft cultures, traditions, and types of magick and take note of the one(s) that 'speak' or make sense to you; for example, if you are an avid gardener then you might be drawn to a type of green related witchcraft. Another thing that you can read about connects with my next tip: your hobbies.

Take a closer look at your hobbies and your interests, they could point you in the right direction. Spend a lot of time around plants? Again, you might be some kind of green witch. Do you like going to the beach just to be around the water? Or even like going to lakes and rivers? You might be a sea witch. But don't get too lost in looking for connections, just step back and list your top favorite activities you do the most often and take it from there.

Now for this next tip, have you ever considered using your own astrological sign for more than just your horoscope? Using your own astrological reading from your natal chart can possibly determine where your path lies. However, I'm not talking about just using your sun sign to possibly determine your path, both your moon and ascending signs are equally important for consideration. Below I give you a brief summary for each of the signs and what kind of witchcraft that they may be connected with:

- Aries: Possesses fiery energy and is assertive and passionate. Possible connection to Warrior Witches.

- Taurus: Very grounded and patient, yet determined. Possible connection to Cottage Witches (a variation of the Green Witch path).

- Gemini: Can be restless and extremely active, sometimes they feel divided or indecisive of their spirituality. Possible connection to Hedge Witches.

- Cancer: Are caring and sensitive. The Moon is at home in this sign, so Cancers tend to feel emotions deeply and are in tune with the lunar cycle, so they hold a possible deep connection to Lunar Witches.

- Leo: Are creative and outgoing, but can also be dramatic, is ruled by the sun and so they have a possible connection to Solar Witches.

- Virgo: Are practical and perfectionistic but do have a close connection to the earth, and so they have a possible connection to Garden Witches.

- Libra: Libras are sociable and crave beauty, they are very creative and all of these traits combined can lead to those with this sign along a path of being an Art Witch.

- Scorpio: Tend to be misunderstood. They have a reputation of being possessive and secretive, but are also capable of wisdom and great transformation. They aren't afraid of 'dark' subjects; they have possible connections to Shadow Witches.

- Sagittarius: Are adventurous and optimistic but can be a little restless as they are always seeking knowledge and understanding. They have a possible connection to Wild Witches.

- Capricorn: Are ambitious and reliable, but are also conservative, reserved, and value traditions. They have a possible connection to Kitchen Witches.

- Aquarius: Are independent and rebellious but can also seem detached. They can also be deeply political as this is the sign of social revolutions, while also having a connection with astrology, hence why there is a possible connection to Astro Witches.

- Pisces: Pisces is one of the most deeply intuitive signs. They are dreamy and imaginative but that can lead to them being unrealistic; however, their intuition can lead to a possible connection to Empath Witches.

But don't make the mistake of these being written in stone, remember that there are other factors out in the world and within yourself that help you determine what kind of witch you are!

Another piece of advice I can give you is that you can always try out a particular type of magick to see if it is right for you. What I don't recommend is you trying out any advanced or group spell or ritual. First, trying a few basic spells or rituals based on a tradition that you are interested in is a good way to see if you are a good fit with it. You should start with the basics because you don't want to accidentally summon a force that you aren't equipped to handle, such as a god or goddess that you don't have a proper setup for. They are forces that should never be toyed with and could prove to be detrimental to you in some way.

Start off with a spell or ritual that is small, such as crystal healing or basic herb work as you are connecting with nature rather than specific deities and aren't as likely to impact you negatively should something go awry.

The last tip I have for you is for you not to be scared of mixing magick around. While some forms of witchcraft have strict and formal traditions, for the most part, different forms of witchcraft do mesh well with others. Don't hesitate to experiment, don't limit yourself on what kind of magick is in your path.

Wheel of the Year

The Wheel of the Year refers to the annual turning of the seasons and helps us to reconnect with the Earth and the essence of our existence. Unlike the 'Gregorian' calendar that is the standard, where the New Year is on January 1st and we track monthly, the wheel instead follows the seasons.

It does this by marking the path that Earth takes around the sun, which of course in ancient times was mistaken to be vice-versa, and marking the changes in the world. There are eight major holidays in the wheel, called Sabbats, and are considered "days of power" because those are particularly powerful times to perform our magick.

Four of the Sabbats are called "solar holidays" and are known as the Summer and Winter Solstices, and the Spring and Autumn Equinoxes—although they are referred to by different names which we will get to in a moment. The other four Sabbats are called the "Earth festivals" and occur between the solar Sabbats.

In addition, there are also monthly rituals that mark the lunar cycle, these are called Esbats and some people refer to them as being the 'second' wheel of the year. Esbats honor the moon and the Goddess, while the Sabbats honor the God and the sun. Below are brief details of the Sabbats and the Esbats:

SABBATS

YULE

(Winter Solstice, December 20-23)

Considered by most traditions as the beginning of a new year, Yule celebrates the rebirth of the God, and as the shortest day of the year, it is a reminder that even though the cold season is getting started, it isn't going to last forever. This time is used to prepare for a quiet, inner focus as the Earth is resting from her hard work.

IMBOLC

(February 2)

Imbolc is celebrated as the first stirrings of spring after those seemingly long winter months. It symbolizes the Goddess beginning to recover after the birth of the God and the days growing longer are a sign of the God gaining power. This time is used for ritual cleansing after such a long period of inactivity; covens can also use this Sabbat as a time for initiation rituals, as it is a time of new beginnings.

OSTARA

(Spring Equinox, March 19-21)

At this time, light and dark are equal and the growth of the earth speeds up as the light from the still young

God and the Goddess' fertility become more powerful. Gardening begins with enthusiasm and trees blossom, because night and day are equal. This is considered a good time for balancing and bringing harmony to opposing forces.

BELTANE

(May 1)

As this is the time that spring moves into summer, the Goddess is changing into the Mother aspect of herself and the God matures into his full potency. It is at this time that the God and Goddess couple to ensure his rebirth at Yule after his death at the end of the life cycle. Fertility is high and the earth is about to bloom with new life. This is a festival of celebrating love, sex, and reproduction.

LITHA

(Summer Solstice, June 20-22)

Litha is one of the most magickal times of the year and is the time where the God and Goddess are at their full power. As the sun is at its highest point and the days are the longest, this is a time for celebrating the abundance of sunlight and warmth.

LAMMAS

(August 1)

This Sabbat marks the beginning of the harvest season, where the crops are brought in from the fields, and the plants and trees drop their fruit. The days grow shorter as the Gods' powers begin to fade; it is the time to give thanks for the abundance of the growing season.

MABON

(Autumn Equinox, September 21-24)

This Sabbat still focuses on the harvest season, the animals born during the year have matured and the trees are starting to lose their leaves, so we are all preparing for the coming winter. The God is preparing to leave the physical plane and the days and nights are equal in length once again, so like the Spring Equinox, nature is in balance, with no season lasting forever and neither dark nor light overpowers the other.

SAMHAIN

(October 31)

Many consider this to be the most important of the Sabbats, Samhain is the time when death is remembered and honored. This is when the God retreats into the shadows and is a reminder of the sacrifices made throughout the year to survive the upcoming winter. Some people consider Samhain to be the beginning of the year as the death and rebirth aspects of creation are intertwined at this time.

ESBATS

Compared to Sabbats, Esbats are celebrated monthly, where ritual and magick are performed, typically during the month's full moon, although some traditions do honor the new moon instead. For this book I will be giving the traditional names of each month's full moons that are seen within the Wheel of the Year, who have their own seasonal attributions in addition to their names. The names themselves vary from differing traditions but they are generally related to the seasons that they happen in. The following are the typical names given in the Northern Hemisphere:

- January: Cold/Hunger/Wolf Moon

- February: Quickening/Snow/Wild Moon

- March: Crow/Sap/Seed/Storm Moon

- April: Hare/Pink/Wind Moon

- May: Flower/Merry/Milk Moon

- June: Lover's/Mead/Rose/Strawberry/Strong Sun/Sun Moon

- July: Blessing/Thunder Moon
- August: Corn/Grain/Red Moon
- September: Harvest/Singing Moon
- October: Blood/Falling Leaf/Hunter's Moon
- November: Beaver/Frost/Mourning Moon
- December: Long Nights/Winter Moon

Many witches also consider astrological influences and will work around what astrological sign the full moon is in and refer to it by the sign, such as "Virgo Moon" or "Libra Moon." More information on how the moon can enhance your power will be covered momentarily, but first we will delve more deeply into the elements.

THE ELEMENTS

Much of the way that we connect with the energies of the universe is when we are communing with the elements in one way or another; there are a few ways other than spellcasting and rituals to connect with the elements and help enhance our powers. Before we get into all of that, I will go over the four (or sometimes five) elements that we have around us.

EARTH

Earth represents the "solid" state of matter, it is the manifestation of things that are constant and durable. Earth is the element that we are closest to as we are made of the earth, which makes us a part of our own world. This is the element that you would call upon if you wanted to build upon a new aspect of your life or to ground yourself. The element of earth is connected to the zodiac signs of Taurus, Virgo, and Capricorn. If you are one of these signs, then you should maintain the connection to yourself by performing earth rituals on a regular basis as it will help you stay grounded and centered.

FIRE

If earth is the element that is closest to us, then fire is the most powerful as it is capable of changing the other elements. Fire is the manifestation of heat and is also the most visible energy. Fire is the constant change in matter so long as it is lit; it is the element that excites and incites our souls and is called upon to bring us active change. The element of fire is connected to the zodiac signs of Aries, Leo, and Sagittarius. If you are one of these signs then using fire rituals will help you stay strong and vibrant.

AIR

Where fire is the element that changes and transforms other elements, air is the element that is always changing and represents the "gas" state of matter, making it dynamic and mobile. Not to mention that the air we breathe is essential to our lives despite not being able to see it. Air is the element we call upon to both move and stimulate change. It is connected to the zodiac signs of Gemini, Libra, and Aquarius. If you are one of these signs then using rituals connected with air will help maintain your great communication skills and brilliant selves.

WATER

Water is the "liquid" state of matter, and like air, is essential to the continued existence of all life. In fact the very blood that flows through not just our bodies, but the bodies of our animal companions, is simply water with some minerals flowing along with it. Water cleans and washes away what is no longer needed, however it is the opposite of earth as it lacks stability. Even when frozen into ice, it will still melt, and similarly to air, water is also constantly changing. Water is extremely important and is used to bless and clean in some rituals, such as releasing rituals. The element of water is connected to the zodiac signs of Cancer, Scorpio, and Pisces. If you are one of these signs then using water rituals will help you stay connected to your creative and sensitive souls.

Remember that the elements are only a few layers of meaning that you add to your rituals. They are only part of the energies that work to change your life by influencing it, much like the Sabbats. Phases of the moon can also help empower your rituals.

The Power of the Moon

I doubt that there was ever a time when humanity hasn't been fascinated by the moon, spending time just staring at the night sky in the hopes of seeing that glowing ball of celestial beauty. That fascination has yet to wane with humanity. In addition to the sun being the brightest star in the sky and the source of life, the moon is the other brightest light in the sky with an influence over many aspects of life, such as our ocean tides and crop growths. Its lunar power also has a large influence over our craft as well.

Like the Sabbats, certain phases of the moon can add an extra boost of power to certain desires behind their spells and rituals. I will teach you about which phases can aid in different ways. This doesn't mean that you can't cast certain spells or perform certain rituals anytime you want, it is simply more helpful to be able to act upon them during these certain phases. I will start by touching upon the phase that is important to the Esbats.

FULL MOON

When the moon is full, it means that the moon is in her full glory and is therefore at her most powerful, hence why Esbats fall during a full moon. It isn't only Esbat related magick that will benefit from being performed during a full moon. It is a time of strength; the perfect time to clean our ritual tools, such as our tarot decks and scrying mirror to name a few, and to honor the moon goddess.

As for the types of spells and rituals that are best performed on a full moon, they include: enhancing your psychic abilities, advancing in your career and work, increasing your self-confidence, strengthening your bonds with family and friends, and anything to do with good luck spells and love. One last thing to note is that the best time to cast love spells is when the full moon falls on a Friday.

WANING MOON

This moon phase is great for casting spells and performing rituals by drawing strength from the universe to help dispel any negative energies that may be latching onto us. If you are around difficult people or situations and you have trouble coping, then this is the best time to call upon the moon for aid.

As for the types of spells and rituals that are best performed when the moon is waning, they include ones that help develop your inner strength, banishing enemies, removing yourself from tricky situations, and calming your anxiety.

NEW MOON

While the full moon is the most powerful phase for spells, the new moon has unique magick in its own in that it is a great time for new beginnings, whether it is starting a new romance, planting a garden, starting a new business, or even some kind of creative endeavor.

The types of spells and rituals that are best performed during a new moon include: career changes (in contrast to advancements during the full moon), moving homes easily, safe travel, and even requesting for better health.

WAXING MOON

The waxing moon is the perfect time for us to improve our situations. It can help give the boost that is required to kick start a much needed change to get things moving in the right direction if they have been stuck in a rut for a while.

The types of spells and rituals that are best performed when the moon is waxing include: moving forward from depression, passing tests and exams, finding lost items, healing pets or finding ones that have been lost, losing weight, and to stop smoking.

I've spent this entire opening chapter talking about drawing energy from other sources, whether it is the elements, the moon, or even the holidays. What I have yet to talk to you about is the energy that comes from within.

How to Work with Energy

All life has energy, whether it comes from the earth, emits from our deities, or in the case of this lesson, our personal power. Our personal energy is very important when it comes to practicing our craft as it helps us in our ability to feel and 'read' it to better understand our surroundings, be in tune with nature's cycles, and even to receive psychic information, but you must believe in its existence or at least have an open mind if you really want to feel and use it.

So why am I talking about it as a first lesson? In many traditions, it is not only recommended, but crucial that you learn how to center, ground, and shield your energy before you begin to work with magick, and I definitely agree with that sentiment. I will now talk briefly about these three techniques and why they are needed to practice properly.

CENTERING

Centering is the foundation of working with energy and magick itself. Centering is the first part of energy work, and if you are a witch who is working with a tradition that is built upon manipulating energy, then learning how to center is something that you need to know. Each tradition has their own definition of centering, depending on your witch type, so in depth research on your own outside of this book is needed to help you find your own way of centering.

GROUNDING

Grounding is a technique you would apply for a few reasons, such as performing a ritual or spell that left you a little wound up afterwards to the point where you can't sleep, or if you didn't center yourself properly, then you might be feeling a little unbalanced. These feelings mean that you have excess energy that needs burning and that is what grounding is for. Grounding is quite simple and there are several ways to do it with the desired result of pushing that unwanted energy away from you into something else. Please exercise caution when grounding your energy as the unwanted energy may accidentally be absorbed by someone else, leaving them unbalanced.

SHIELDING

Shielding is the technique which helps you protect yourself from harm, whether it be magickal, psychic or even mental. It is the opposite of grounding. Where grounding pushes away excess energy, with shielding you use that same energy to surround yourself for protection.

Examples of each of these energy flowing techniques will be given in chapter five.

FROM BELIEF TO PRACTICE

It is one thing to read about what goes into witchcraft, whether it is deciding what witch types we are, finding out what tools we need, or finding any beginner spells that we would be interested in trying. It is another thing entirely to actually practice our magick. Reading is all well and good, it is great to know as much as there is to know in regards to all the basics—the wheel of the year, the elements, etc—however, reading isn't enough, you must actually practice and perform magick in order for it to work.

Reading too much can cause us to suffer from a kind of "analysis paralysis" in which we are unable to make a decision based on overthinking a problem. It's caused by having so much information that we can't decide on how to proceed, whether it is because a moon phase clashes with a particular want or not having a particular herb in season or one of many other things that can hold you back. The end result is that you aren't able to make a decision.

While there is no such thing as reading too much, it isn't enough for you to know *about* magickal applications, you must know through *actual* practice of the craft. But if you do end up suffering from analysis paralysis, then you need to realize that there is a problem, take a step back, and think about how to solve it. Perhaps you can seek advice from someone, understand the exact problem, and then set a deadline for yourself to help you decide what you don't need to include in your rituals and spells. Remember, witchcraft isn't an intellectual practice!

Witchcraft is a spiritual practice, which means that the intent behind rituals and spells are necessary for them to come to pass. Because they are focused and purposeful communications with the energies of creation, it doesn't matter if they are practiced by a group of witches or by a solitary one; no one is more or less powerful than the other.

So when you are ready to begin practicing, you can follow the steps that I outline throughout the next subsequent chapters, beginning with chapter three, which discusses a witch's toolkit. First, we will discuss how to use witchcraft in your everyday life.

Chapter 2

Modern Witchcraft

So what does it mean to be a modern practicing witch? And how does it differ from times gone by? That is what I will be going over with you in this chapter and I'll first talk about how to think like a modern day witch.

Modern times seem to be a bit hectic don't they? There's always places to go, people to meet, and things to do. At times, we barely have time to eat and sleep, never mind finding the time to practice our craft. But that's just how it looks on the surface, by digging a little deeper, you'll realize that there are advantages these days that make practicing our craft easier than ever.

The most prominent advantage is the internet, which allows learning to be more accessible. You just need to be careful, because while there is helpful information online, there can also be a bit of misinformation too that can lead you down the wrong road. Even better, we can now use it to order any supplies that we would require for our magick, whether it be herbs, crystals, or objects for our altars.

One thing that would be considered 'modern' is the use of the word 'witch' in that it doesn't always refer to a female practitioner. The word can be used to refer to any gender of magick users, although some males may prefer the term 'wizard' and some might prefer another term like 'magician' or 'warlock' over 'witch,' and that is perfectly fine.

Another thing to remember is that witches come in different shapes and sizes because despite what the Halloween decorations might say, witches don't wear pointed hats or ride broomsticks. Witches come from all walks of life—they can be doctors, lawyers, and even janitors; it's quite likely that you regularly walk past fellow witches on the street without realizing it.

But what hasn't changed are the foundations of morality upon which our practice is based. In the introduction I touched on the fact that witchcraft isn't an organized religion. We're far too diverse and independent in our practices to be considered such a thing. However, we still have some basic principles that all magick practitioners share in regards to what we can believe, what we can do, and what we can't (or rather shouldn't) do. I've listed some examples of a modern witch's dos and don'ts below.

WE DO

BELIEVE IN "THE THREEFOLD LAW": Just because witches don't have a police force to tell them that they are misusing their magick doesn't mean that we are off the hook if we are using it for ill-gotten reasons. The Threefold Law means that whatever you put out into the world, for good or bad, will come back at you three times. But don't get hung up on what threefold means, if it is three separate times or three times strong; the point is that like attracts like, if you put good out into the universe you will receive the same in return.

BELIEVE IN THE "WICCAN REDE": This is a line of ethics that says: "An' it harm none, do as you will" and is considered the Wiccan "Golden Rule." Like the previous point, the rule simply says that you don't deliberately harm anyone, but that also includes harming yourself by not celebrating life as you should.

WE DON'T

USE WITCHCRAFT TO GAIN POWER OVER OTHERS: We use witchcraft to develop our own powers.

IT'S NOT JUST ABOUT THE MAGICK: Adding to the above point, witchcraft is so much more than simply learning a few spells. It's about understanding and respecting the energies.

BE EXCLUSIVE WITH BELIEFS: There is nothing in the practice of witchcraft that says their practitioners have to subscribe to a singular belief or tradition.

HAVE A BLACK AND WHITE VIEW: We witches see shades of gray in our lives and dualities in our practice, so a view like this is limiting and unwelcome.

TREAT IT LIKE A TREND: It's one thing to be a witch who dresses alternatively or even has tattoos, but getting into witchcraft for reasons like because it seems trendy or for reasons like you're attempting to intimidate people does nothing but trivialize what it truly means to be a witch.

TRY TO CONVERT OTHERS: To me this is a big one, witchcraft is about choosing to practice the magick, not because we were forced into it. While it's fun to share what we know with people that are interested, we certainly are never to force others to 'convert' into it if they choose not to pursue witchcraft in the end.

However, how a witch is to behave is only a part of what it means to be a modern witch. We also have a small arsenal of practical magick practices that are a lot easier to use than way back when. Let us go over them right now.

Practical Magick

Auras

You've likely heard the term 'aura' tossed around, but what exactly is an aura? Simply put, an aura refers to a seven layered luminous body that encompasses your physical one and presents itself as nets of energy. Any problems that are occurring in each layer are caught up in these nets. Auras are kind of the same as 'vibes,' short for "vibrational frequency," which is what auras are made of. The seven layers match the colors of the rainbow, which are detailed here:

RED: Energetic, strong-willed, and well-grounded

ORANGE: Adventurous, considerate, and thoughtful

YELLOW: Creative, friendly, and relaxed

GREEN: Communicator, nurturing, and social

BLUE: Freethinker, intuitive, and spiritual

INDIGO: Curious, gentle, and spiritually connected

VIOLET: Independent, intellectual, and wise

Each layer also corresponds with an additional meaning:

PHYSICAL: The layer that is connected with our physical comforts, health, and the five senses; it might be diminished when we're awake and revitalized when we're resting.

ASTRAL: This is the emotional layer tied to our sensitive nature, and where we provide ourselves with self-love.

LOWER MENTAL: This is likely the layer that we use most frequently because it is thought to be where reason and thought patterns are; this layer is used to study, work, focus, and execute your personal beliefs and values.

HIGHER MENTAL: This layer connects our ability to care for ourselves and for others; it is thought to serve as a bridge in between the other layers.

SPIRITUAL: This layer allows us the possibility of connecting with other people over spiritual matters; doing so is thought to cause this layer to shine brighter.

INTUITIONAL: This is the layer that is said to be your "third eye" (more on that later), this layer is thought to help you see your dreams and be more aware of your intuition and instincts.

ABSOLUTE: This last layer is thought to act as a binder, in which it keeps the other layers confined to you and living in harmony.

The auras colors also correspond with one of the seven main chakras, as detailed below.

CHAKRAS

Chakra refers to the energy points in your body, and is a system that is both ancient and complex. Translating as 'wheel,' they are thought to be spinning disks of energy that should remain 'open' and aligned as they are attached to parts of our bodies that affect our physical and emotional well-being. Here are the main seven chakras, along with their corresponding color, location, and meaning, of the possible one hundred and fourteen chakras. They run along our spines and are what we typically refer to when talking about our chakras.

ROOT

- **Color:** Red
- **Location:** Base of spine, tailbone area
- **Meaning:** Grounding, physical identity, stability

Sacral

- **Color:** Orange
- **Location:** Below belly button, just above pubic bone
- **Meaning:** Creativity, pleasure, sexuality

Solar Plexus

- **Color:** Yellow
- **Location:** Upper abdomen, stomach area
- **Meaning:** Confidence, self-esteem

Heart

- **Color:** Green
- **Location:** Center of chest, just above heart
- **Meaning:** Compassion, love

Throat

- **Color:** Blue
- **Location:** Throat
- **Meaning:** Communication

Brow/Third Eye

- **Color:** Indigo
- **Location:** Between eyes, on the forehead
- **Meaning:** Imagination, intuition

CROWN

- **Color:** Violet or white
- **Location:** Very top of head
- **Meaning:** Awareness, intelligence

When the seven chakras are in balance, your body is in harmony. However, when they are unbalanced in some way, they can affect the area they are associated with and if that is the case, then they have to be unblocked. This can be done through exercises such as yoga postures and meditation, as well as breathing practices that encourage the flow of energy. Here are some sample yoga poses for each chakra and a brief summary as to why the pose is beneficial.

MOUNTAIN POSE: Root Chakra. This pose connects us to the earth's energy and invites it upward throughout the entire body.

REVOLVED TRIANGLE POSE: Sacral Chakra. Stimulates the abdominal organs to promote energy circulation.

BOAT POSE: Solar Plexus Chakra. Activates your core and internal fire to aid in alignment.

LOW LUNGE: Heart Chakra. Invites the heart to open for alignment.

Easy Pose with Chanting: Throat Chakra. The chanting helps with alignment and to open the chakra.

Dolphin Pose: Third Eye Chakra. Increases circulation to our faces and brains.

Balancing Butterfly: Crown Chakra. Invites balance, concentration, and peace for alignment.

There is an additional way that may surprise you and that is healing crystals, as detailed below.

CRYSTALS

Crystals have fascinated us over a period of centuries for various reasons. Whether it is being worn as beautiful jewelry or for our purposes in the differing vibrational energies that help us to heal with our ailments related to our bodies, minds, and emotions. So long as you cleanse your crystals properly and have the ones that vibrate with you, your healing crystals will help to stabilize whichever part of your body is giving you trouble.

One way that crystals help you is to balance out your chakras. Below is a short list of crystals connected to one or more chakras:

Root: Apache Tears, Lodestone, Obsidian

Sacral: Aventurine (orange), Carnelian (brown-orange), Topaz (peach)

Solar Plexus: Citrine, Jasper (brown or yellow), Tigers Eye (yellow)

Heart: Emerald, Peridot, Rose Quartz

Throat: Chalcedony, Lapis Lazuli, Turquoise

Brow/Third Eye: Jade (purple), Moonstone, Sapphire (blue or pink)

Crown: Calcite (white), Howlite, Opal (white or colorless)

Any chakra: Agate (all, depending on color), Ametrine (solar plexus, third eye, crown), Kyanite (all, depending on color)

However, crystals can just be lucky, or used as representation for the element on earth, more on this will be discussed in the next chapter.

DREAM INTERPRETATION

Dreaming is admittedly difficult to explain. One such explanation originates from the belief of many ancient peoples, such as the Egyptians and the Greeks, who considered them to be a form of supernatural communication or divine intervention. These ancient peoples relied on those who had an association with spiritual powers to interpret them.

However, what makes dreams tricky is that the images that come to us could have more than one meaning, that is if we even remember them at all upon awakening. A dream that comes to us could simply be something our subconscious mind had conjured up because of something good or bad in our conscious mind. But in other cases, dreams can tell us of events or things that haven't happened yet or are not yet in our control.

Another thing that may hinder us from knowing their meanings is that dreams aren't always literal—if anything they rarely are—so if you happen to dream of falling off a cliff or of your teeth falling out, chances are they are simply metaphorical pictures. Despite these obstacles, it is beneficial for us to understand our dreams as they can give us realizations about how we think and feel, which in turn provides us with personal insight. But how do we interpret our dreams?

One way is to think hard about what is going on in our lives currently. However, that may prove difficult as there may be multiple things going on in your life. So how are you to separate one from another? The answer may lie in having dream dictionaries on hand. As there is a possibility of multiple subjects having more than one meaning, your best bet is at least two or three dream dictionaries on hand so you can cross compare.

As for the amount of symbols that have been interpreted, there are dictionaries out there that boast having over 12,000!

For now we will look at a small sample of dreams you might have dreamed of in the past. Below are nine common dreams and a short interpretation of each of them.

BEING CHASED: In general, being chased in a dream means you are trying to avoid something in your daily life. What that may be depends a little on who/what is pursuing you. If an animal is chasing you, you may be hiding from passion, anger, or other feelings. If an unknown pursuer is chasing you, this may relate to a past trauma or childhood experience. If a member of the opposite sex is chasing you, this may indicate you may be afraid of love or are haunted by a previous relationship.

DYING: These reflect your anxiety about some kind of change, or you are afraid of the unknown.

FALLING: These dreams are a sign that there is an aspect of your life that isn't going too well; it is a suggestion to rethink a choice or consider a new direction in your life.

FLYING: There are two different interpretations, the first might reflect feelings of freedom and independence, but the other could be a sign that you are wanting to escape or flee from life's realities.

INFIDELITY: Could be a reflection of your fear of a partner being unfaithful, but could also be a manifestation of issues with trust, loyalty, and communication in a relationship.

LOSING TEETH: Has more than one meaning. You could be worried about your appearance, or your communication skills, or the concern that you have said something embarrassing.

NAKED IN PUBLIC: These dreams might be an indication of you feeling like a phony or feeling afraid of revealing your shortcomings and imperfections.

PREGNANCY: This one has a wide range of possibilities, from creativity to fear. Sometimes these dreams may represent a woman fearing she will not be a good mother, other times they may suggest you are developing a deepening or potential relationship.

TAKING A TEST: Reveals a fear of failure or of being unprepared.

OPENING THE THIRD EYE

When we talk about the "third eye," we are of course talking about the third eye chakra that is also sometimes called the "brow" chakra briefly covered above. The third eye chakra is related to clarity, concentration, imagination, intuition, spiritual perception, and universal connection; opening your third eye is said to provide us with insight, wisdom, and the deepening of our spiritual connection. On the other hand, if your third eye chakra is blocked then you can run into problems such as confusion, cynicism, lack of purpose, pessimism, and uncertainty. So how do you open your third eye? There are a few methods touched on below:

ACTIVATION

The third eye is directly connected to the pineal gland[1]. You can use your circadian rhythm to activate your third eye, by focusing on thoughts of thanks for your intuitive abilities and for your connection to nature.

DIET

Diet can in fact play a role in opening your third eye. There are several foods that can support and detoxify the third eye:

- Cilantro
- Coconut Oil
- Garlic
- Ginseng
- Goji Berries

---

[1] A small pea-shaped gland in the brain at the base of the skull that secretes the hormone melatonin and helps to regulate circadian rhythms.

- Hemp Seeds
- Honey
- Lemon
- Raw Cacao
- Star Anise
- Vitamin D3
- Watermelon

Essential Oils

Essential oils are good for opening and healing your third eye. There are three that are recommended: jasmine, lemon, and sandalwood. In addition, here are steps to make a blend for your third eye.

1. Take one or more of these oils, as well as a carrier oil (an oil that dilutes to make it safer to put essential oils on your skin).

2. Mix them together, using one teaspoon of carrier oil for every six drops of essential oil.

3. Apply mixture directly to your third eye chakra.

Please note that some essential oils, especially citrus ones like lemon, can cause sensitivity to light, so you should avoid exposing yourself to the sun after putting citrus oils on your skin. You should also be absolutely sure that you are not allergic to the oils before use.

MEDITATION AND CHANTING

Meditation livens up the pineal gland through vibration and intention. Chanting meditation can help bring up a feeling of appreciation and gratitude.

USING CRYSTALS

Before I touch on the connection between crystals and the healing of the chakras, I will say that crystals make great allies when it comes to opening the third eye. I will also say that the best crystals to use are ones that are on the indigo, purple, and violet color palette.

You can use them by placing the crystal or gemstone on your third eye chakra during meditation or by using a crystal grid.

There is no exact timeframe as to how long it takes for the third eye to open, it could take days, weeks, months, or even longer; it could even take a lifetime of practice to open. But once it is open, you'll notice as you start receiving visions and guidance messages.

TAROT CARDS

Of all the well known modern magickal tools, tarot cards are chief among them. They are seen in movies and TV more often than anything else, even crystals.

Tarot cards are tools that are both powerful and sacred, they are used to direct one's life. So how do we use them? Well, first off, you need a deck. The best recommendation for beginners is the "Rider-Waite" deck that was first published back in 1910 because their imagery is simple, as is their symbolism and

color scheme.

But what is a deck made of? Tarot decks contain 78 cards that are split into two groups: the major arcana and the minor arcana. The easiest way to remember which group is which is to compare to a standard playing card deck. The 22 major arcana are the "trump cards," but don't have suits; they represent significant figures, influences, life events and revelations. Below are the major arcana with their corresponding numbers:

0. The Fool
1. The Magician
2. The High Priestess
3. The Empress
4. The Emperor
5. The Hierophant
6. The Lovers
7. The Chariot
8. Justice
9. The Hermit
10. The Wheel of Fortune
11. Strength
12. The Hanged Man
13. Death
14. Temperance
15. The Devil
16. The Tower
17. The Stars
18. The Moon
19. The Sun
20. Judgment
21. The World

As for the minor arcana, they represent the more everyday and mundane matters of life. There are 56 cards that are divided into four suits: cups, pentacles, wands, and swords (with occasional other terms, depending on the deck).

Each suit represents a different facet of life: cups represent emotion, pentacles are money and work, wands represent creativity and passion, and swords are intellect. In addition, the minor arcana are separated into numbers and "face" cards, which are knave, knight, queen and king. The suits of the cards are also aligned with groupings of astrological signs by the four elements: cups with water, pentacles with earth, wands with fire, and swords with air. However, if you are a beginner, then you don't need to worry about any kind of interpretation except for the basics.

There are a variety of ways to use this deck, how to shuffle, what kind(s) of spreads to use etc. It is up to you to find out how you use your tarot.

Before we end this chapter, we'll touch on one aspect of witchcraft that has lasted from times gone by to the modern-day.

COVENS

A coven refers to a group or gathering of witches. They are groups who typically gather together for rituals, such as celebrating the Sabbats. In the past, you would have to go and search out a coven if you wished to join one, but now with the internet, to seek one out is relatively easy. In many cases, if you can not find something suitable in your local area, it is now possible to join an online coven, where you can all learn, teach, and communicate with one another remotely.

Unlike what TV and movies suggest, being part of a coven doesn't mean that you have to attend meetings wearing dark shrouded robes and a hooded cloak *(unless you want to of course!). If you want to show up (either online or in real life)* in jeans and a t-shirt, do it! It's highly unlikely that there will be any sort of dress code. Covens are a great way to make friends or receive some hands on wisdom, but by no means is joining one mandatory. We touched on solitary witches in the previous chapter, who don't join a coven in their practices.

In the end, it is up to you which path you take: one of solidarity, or one of cooperation.

Chapter 3

THE WITCH'S TOOL KIT

When it comes to actually performing our magick, just having the urge to do it, or the words to cast your spells or perform your rituals isn't enough. Tools are essential to our practices, regardless of what kind of witch you are, and they come in different forms, whether it be knives, candles, herbs or even something that may surprise you. In this chapter we are going to cover the tools in our kits that are either essential or optional.

AMULETS

Compared to lucky charms and talismans, amulets are objects that are carried around for more general purposes and are used to protect their owners from danger in addition to preventing illness and misfortune. Amulets are considered 'passive' as they react to the events of life rather than creating anything specific. However, while amulets are supposed to provide protection, there are times when the opposite happens and they make life more dangerous—the Hope Diamond[2] is a great example of when amulets go wrong.

Pretty much anything can be a talisman, whether it is something natural like a four-leaf clover, man-made like jewelry, or even specifically made objects.

ALTARS

Not only is having an altar needed to perform our craft, it is a crucial part of our practice. An altar holds it all together, our tools and ingredients. It is the sacred space that is central to our wishes coming to life through our magick!

But what exactly do we put on our altars? You can make up your altar in any way that you please, what matters is that you are comfortable and that you are putting items that are essential to whatever it is you are about to perform. If you are performing a simple tarot card reading then you would just need a deck, but if you are performing a spell or ritual then you would

---

[2] Legend says that after the large blue stone was stolen from an idol in India, bad luck and death would befall anyone who possesses or even touches the hope diamond.

THE WITCH'S TOOL KIT | 61

need much more. However, despite personal preference being of the utmost importance, there are items that are necessary in worshiping and respecting the forces that we utilize in our practice. That is not the only reason that we utilize tools, our tools are also extensions of ourselves!

Before talking about the actual tools, we should discuss how an altar is set up. Almost anything can be used as an altar, it could be an end table, or a cardboard box or anything in between, so long as it can be used to properly perform magick. You also have the option of choosing an object that can be put away when not in use, however there are advantages to designating a space for magick only.

It is all about intention, as the altar is meant to be a sacred space for your practice. You can make your altar as simple or elaborate as you wish, and you may stand or sit when performing magick. You may choose to cover your altar with a cloth. You may also choose to change the cloth's color depending on planetary aspects for a ritual, current season, or for a factor relating to a specific spell or focus. Also consider the direction that your alter faces. Some witches prefer to face north—just know that those who practice white magick never face west.

The 'standard' altar setup has items relating to the God placed on the right side facing because he is considered the 'active' principle, and the right hand is considered by some as the active hand. The Goddess will be on the left side because she is the 'receptive' principle. As we go along, I will talk about where else you put your tools, if you put them on the altar at all.

ATHAME

Athame has various pronunciations, like a-THAH-may, ah-THAH-me, ah-THAW-may, and ATH-um-ay being the most popular. Regardless of how you personally choose to say it, the athame is our most important tool. It's a double-edged ritual knife that often, but not always, has a black handle, with the two sides symbolizing the God and Goddess who come together; the union of the mundane and spiritual words with the idea being that responsibility comes with power.

It doesn't have to be sharp. It depends on the owner's preference, as it is only used to cut air and energy. In fact, some traditions state that if the athame ever touches blood, it becomes tainted and should be destroyed.

Athames are used to direct and focus energy, especially when drawing the circle or calling up the quarters *(see chapter 5)*. Its most common association is with the element of air and the east quarter, but some consider it associated with fire and the south; either way, it also symbolizes the witches' will.

Athames don't need to be put on the altar, but if you choose to do so, then any side that is comfortable to you is fine.

Bolline

A bolline is a knife that usually has a white handle. It is used to make other tools, cut materials, and carve necessary symbols. Bollines can cut objects such as cords and herbs as well as cut symbols or names into candles, and carve out your wand. In addition to its usual white handle, bollines tend to have curved blades, both which distinguish it from an athame. Like the latter you don't need to keep it on the altar all the time.

Book of Shadows

Your Book of Shadows (BOS) is your personal spell book. Unlike the spell books that are shown on TV and movies which show it already written out, your BOS is what you use to write down your spells and rituals; it's a record of your magick work, your history of successful performances. Whether it is circle work, rituals, spells, or even energy work, it is a journal of your magickal successes. As well as writing down everything that you have cast, along with the results, I recommend that you also record whatever lore or practices you find from your own extended research for future reference.

Say, for example, you find that performing a spell or ritual for harmony is at its most potent during a full moon while it is Virgo, then write that down in your BOS to remember in case such magick was ever needed again. But don't think that this is going to be a quick process. It takes a lot of trial, error, and practice to find out the personal secrets to your magick. It is important that this book inspires you. I recommend that you include happy phrases, poetry, and positive affirmations to help uplift your spirits and focus your mind. Positive affirmations can be just a simple line reminding you to have a great day, or complex like a list of what makes you a great person.

This is an optional item on your altar, but a mandatory thing to have.

BROOM

While we don't fly on these, brooms are an important part of our craft. We use them to prepare a space for working with magick by sweeping away negative influences and spirits; so it is an important tool for managing energy. Do not use the kind of broom that you would buy that's machine made, the kind made of plastic; it's necessary to use a broom that's made of wood and woven with straw, typically found at craft fairs, because those natural materials contain energies of their own.

Take note that you should never use your energy broom for housework, otherwise you will mix up the energies of your home and sacred space. If it helps, keep your ritual broom completely separate from the rest of your household tools.

Candles

Candles are everywhere. They have a variety of uses, from a light source to aromatherapy, but just because they're simple doesn't mean that they aren't powerful; on the contrary, candles have powerful magick of their own. What makes candles so interesting is that in their varying states, candles involve all four elements. When the candle isn't lit, it represents earth. When it comes into contact with fire, which burns brightly, the wax that melts represents water, and the smoke that they emit represents air.

In order to be used, candles must be consecrated, dressed, burned, and chosen correctly; candles aren't a one size fits all type of magick. more information on candle magick will be found in chapter five.

Cauldron

Cauldrons are a symbol of the Goddess, as its shape is representative of the womb and female genitalia. Cauldrons usually have three legs for practicality and mobility. They can be placed onto the left side of your altar if there is room, but don't fret if it isn't on yours, just place it on the floor to the left of your altar. Cauldrons can be used to hold a few different elements, such as in the spring it can hold earth or water, while in winter it can hold fire to symbolize the rebirth of the sun.

Cauldrons can also be customized in regards to their shape. In the spring it could be a fountain filled with flowers; in autumn it can be a hollowed out gourd, you can even customize it uniquely to your own ceremonies. Cauldrons are good for mixing your herbs and essential oils, just make sure that you clean them thoroughly before and after every use. They can also be used for scrying by reading images on the water's surface and even be used to burn paper for spells so the flames can carry your wishes to the gods and goddesses. Do be careful when using fire in any of your practices, make sure that there are no drafts to blow the flames around.

CENSER

A Censer, which is sometimes called a 'thurible,' is an incense burner and represents the elements of air and fire. Your censer should be placed in the center of your altar and is vitally important as it is used to purify your other tools as well as your sacred space. The purpose of the incense is to release energy into your sacred space. However, in order to do that properly, you should always test your incense prior to your rituals in order to ensure that there won't be too much smoke that could cause breathing problems.

If you or someone else finds incense smoke either concerning or irritating, then there are other options for symbolizing air like a fan or feathers.

CHALICE

Chalices are another vessel that symbolizes the Goddess and femininity and is a tool that should be put on your altar. Again it is to be placed on the left side with the rest of the similar representations. It is connected to the element of water. While in use on the altar, it can hold any liquid that has been blessed; it doesn't have to be only water, it can also hold mead, wine, or even juice. It is customary after many rituals and sabbat ceremonies to toast the deities with ale, cider, or wine and thank them for being there. If you are doing an outdoor ritual, you can pour the liquid from the chalice onto the ground as an offering to the benevolent entities around you after you have opened your circle, so long as it is a natural liquid such as water so as to avoid polluting the earth.

Charm Boxes

These are magickal boxes that are used to store magick items that help out with an area that you are lacking, depending upon what you put inside it. One example would be a "hope chest" that women used to have that had intentions, materials, and wishes for a happy marriage. They are easy to make so long as you have the most powerful combinations of ingredients based upon your needs, however a beginner might not wish to attempt one until they are comfortable with their knowledge in regards to their desires. A love box, for example, can contain a pink candle, some rose petals, a couple pieces of rose quartz and maybe a couple of copper pennies (Aphrodite's favorite metal).

Herbs

Herbs are an important natural 'tool' to have when you are living a life of magick. They grow from the earth, have powerful connections to it and each have vibrations of their own that make different herbs suitable for a particular use; some even have connections to various deities. But some herbs are more dangerous to use than others, so careful research is needed before you decide whether or not to use them.

LUCKY CHARMS

Lucky charm qualities are a combination of amulets and talismans. They are generalized like the former and active like the latter; they are intended to attract good fortune and luck by their users.

MAGICK BOTTLES

Magick bottles, which are also called "Spell Jars," help empower us in addition to having more decorative purposes, so they are like charm boxes this way. But unlike the boxes, magick in the bottles is active depending on not just what you put in it, but where you put it. Bottles put outside can keep your plants healthy, bottles on your mantel can help protect your home, love and happiness next to your bed, etc. You can also customize your bottles with crystal stoppers. You can make your own magick bottles by filling them with symbolic objects of your desire and inscribing on the lid or cork top your sigil of choice.

One example of a bottle is one that's used for improving luck with money. You fill the bottle with three pennies and either some jade or pyrite and put it in your workspace; whenever you think about your finances, just shake the bottle and your situation should improve in three days.

Magick Cord

This is a rope that binds you to magick. It's typically nine feet long and should be made of red ribbon or wool and is braided and tied into a loop at one end to symbolize feminine energy and left loose at the other to symbolize male energy. If you choose to braid your own cord, you start with a braid of three strands that are fourteen feet long to get the nine feet after braiding. If you want to enhance your cord's power, you can weave crystal beads in the strands—clear quartz works best as they are energy amplifiers.

Mirrors

Mirrors aren't just to check to see if a strand of hair is out of place, they are a good scrying tool as well as they are shiny, smooth, and reflective. You can make your own scrying mirror and empower it in a few different ways: first you can find a round mirror with a frame that will make it easy to glue things onto it like crystals or seashells, such as wood or plastic.

Make sure to clean your frame with a soft, dry cloth, before you apply glue that dries clear, then put on your desired items one at a time in any pattern you want. Just remember that different scrying querying may require different mirrors for different requests. Here are a couple of examples of the meaning to small objects that can be glued to the mirror:

- Jade: Relates to money matters
- Rubies: Love matters

More examples of scrying tools are below.

SCRYING TOOLS

Scrying has been used since the pre-biblical times. It is thought that the oldest scrying tool was a piece of black obsidian, possibly used by a Stone Age shaman. When they are used, not only can you divine the past, present, and future, you can also contact spirit guides and even improve your skills of creative visualization. Some practitioners use it as a gateway to the astral plane.

The typical scrying tool has a shiny surface, but you can scry with almost anything, whether it is water, a mirror, even flames, or a bowl of ink is used.

Crystal Balls

Another staple with a long history of magickal practice — thousands of years' worth — are balls made from beryl or quartz crystals which are used for divination. Choosing a crystal ball for yourself isn't something to be taken lightly. This is a very personal tool that will contain your energy. They also have their own power and they can have an influence on the development of our psychic abilities.

Crystal balls are basically containers that house your energy, which is why it is important that you only have one that feels right for you. It should also be comfortable for you to hold, not too heavy, nor too light. Because it's yours, you shouldn't allow anyone else to touch it, but if someone does, then you cleanse it by leaving it in a bowl of sea salt overnight.

Statues

Many witches have statues that represent the God and Goddess and whatever deity that they are worshiping and calling upon, but they aren't essential. However, having them can enhance the spiritual atmosphere.

Talismans

The whole point of a talisman is to give out powers, encouragement, protection, and energy to its owner and is created specifically for that purpose. They can be made from almost any material, like metal, stone, or parchment, and are often inscribed with pictures or words. They are created at certain times which are cosmically or spiritually significant to provide the energy and power that is used by their owners. In fact, it's the owners themselves that make the most powerful ones.

Talismans can be made for both positive and negative uses, but it would be very unwise to create a negative talisman deliberately.

Wand

Wands are no doubt the most well-known witches' tool besides the brooms and spell books, yet they are an important tool nonetheless and differ from the stereotypical usage portrayed in the media. Like athames, they are used to cast circles and bring up deities as it focuses, directs, and projects energy. As they both gather and store magickal energy, wands are great for healing and can be used to 'draw' the shape when you cast the circle.

When it comes to finding your wand, you can bring it to yourself through attraction, just take a walk through the woods and look for sticks that have been dropped from the trees; you could cut a branch off a tree, but I strongly advise against this, especially if you are a baby witch as you would have to give thanks and placate any beings living in the tree and if you do it wrong then they might take offense and create trouble for you; however some witches still choose to thank a tree even if it is a fallen branch by leaving a gift of water or compost at the tree's base.

You can purchase a wand if it suits you. However, purchasing one leaves little room for personalizing it with customizations, and unless you happen to find one that is exactly what you wanted, it would be a shame to just settle. As for how you can make your own wand if you do find that one stick you gravitate toward, there's almost no limit to what you can do with it.

The common woods used for a wand are ash, cherry, oak, and willow; they are also at least a foot long. You can carve symbols that are special to you, and even affix crystals, jewels, and metals onto it that are meaningful. Here are some possible suggestions for crystals to affix onto your wand:

- Amber: Grounding
- Bloodstone: Abundance and prosperity

- Garnet: Protection from gossip
- Rose Quartz: Love

Wands are associated with fire and south because of the wands' use of directing energy, but some witches associate it with air and east because of trees being able to transform carbon dioxide to oxygen through photosynthesis.

Now that we have gone over the common physical tools that witches use for the craft, we will move onto the spiritual tools which are another important part of magick: the symbols and runes that help connect us to magick itself.

Chapter 4

RUNES AND SYMBOLS

You may not realize it, but there are powerful symbols everywhere in our lives. We may see signs in nature that inspire us, or a word or a picture, or something like a logo that is based around an actual symbol, whether it is known or not.

But why are symbols so important in our craft? It's because symbols in themselves are potent, we can see them all around us in the world, they can bring up intense emotions, feelings, and can help us build a solid foundation of ourselves. Symbols are an outside sign of energy that has developed from within us; they are powered by complex intentions that are just condensed into a few lines and shapes.

But, how are they to be used? Firstly, don't panic if the answer doesn't come to you right away, there is no singular 'right' way to invoke their powers; the main thing to remember when using symbols is that it must feel comfortable or right for you. Relax and think about what symbols mean in your mind and let their own meanings reveal themselves. They can be inscribed in ritual items such as candles and the earth itself with a knife or pointed object. They can be written with ink in your own magick books or sketch them out on a paper surface for daily practice. They can also be formed using layouts on your altar or within your circle using items such as candles, crystals, herbs, and tea leaves.

In this chapter, we are going to focus on some common symbols and how they can be used in your craft. We'll look at both the positive uses that I recommend and the negative uses to watch for and avoid. Firstly, let's discuss one of the more commonly used symbol types, Runes.

RUNES

If you're a fan of fantasy novels such as *Where the Forest Meets the Stars* by Glendy Vanderah, you may occasionally run into the use of 'runes,' which are used in a variety of ways. Runes are used for spellcasting the majority of the time, which is all well and good for a fictional setting, however in our world runes aren't quite used that way.

While it's true that runes are symbols that can be used in divination and to answer questions about your life, there is more to it. Runes themselves refer to a collection of materials that have sacred symbols inscribed on them; such as wood pieces, crystals, and even animal bones.

The origin of the word 'rune' isn't totally clear. The accepted explanation is that it's likely to come from the word *run*, which is very old Proto-Germanic and translates as 'mystery', 'secret,' or 'whisper.'

There is no single origin for where runes originate because the evidence shows that they have been used across the world. Norse legends claim that it was Odin himself that discovered them, but the modern explanation is that they come from even earlier script like Etruscan and mixed with the symbols of Teutonic shamans. Regardless of where they came from, runes were first used in the first or second centuries of the Common Era by the Germanic peoples, or the Gothic, Suebian, or Teutonic peoples.

Now, runes in modern times aren't limited by a user's ethnicity or nationality, particularly since modern Germanic languages include English, German, and even Afrikaans, to name a few. The use of runes is as a divination and as a magick tool by having us let our minds focus on our goals and the possible outcomes.

However, there are several different rune alphabets. Some use the same runes but give them different meanings which can make it feel quite confusing at first. I recommend focusing on one rune alphabet at a time until you know it by heart. I'll give a brief overview of the twelve runic alphabets that are available for you to learn:

- ANGLO-SAXON RUNES: These runes have up to thirty-three characters and are one of the hardest runes to learn as a result. This set is an expansion on the Elder Futhark set and was more likely used for writing purposes rather than divination and to include more phonetic sounds as more people adopted them as a means of writing. If you are willing to learn them, then it is best that you learn them after you have mastered the Elder Futhark.

- ARMANEN RUNES: These runes are from the modern times and at one point in their history, they served as an example of how rune magick can be turned around to be used for evil purposes as these runes were used by Nazi Germany as symbols on their uniforms among other uses. However, that does not mean that runes, even this alphabet, are evil themselves, it is how they are used that's important.

- DALECARLIAN RUNES: This runic alphabet that came into existence around the same time as Latin letters. It is an expansion of Medieval Runes as well as both the Elder and Younger

Futhark Runes, which would change drastically when mixed with several other alphabets. These runes are not used for divination purposes.

- DOTTED RUNES: These are runes from the Viking Age that expanded on the Younger Futhark by adding dotted characters and are used as a script and not as divination.

- ELDER FUTHARK RUNES: The oldest runic alphabet in existence, consisting of twenty-four characters and is the best for beginners to learn. They are the most commonly used system for divination; they can also be used to help learn other rune forms as many of them are expansions of this alphabet.

- FRISIAN RUNES: An expansion of the Elder Futhark that has twenty-eight runes; this marks the change of 'futhark' to 'futhork' because a new fourth rune was added that changed the sound.

- GOTHIC RUNES: Named for the Northern European people, the Goths, who adopted this system of twenty-five letters that can be used for divination and has influences from Greek deities.

- MARCOMANNIC RUNES: This system is a mixture of two separate runic alphabets: Elder Futhark and Anglo-Saxon. There are altogether twenty-nine runes in this hybrid alphabet. In my opinion, there really isn't much reason to use Marcomannic Runes for divination unless you fully understand each rune and its meaning.

- MEDIEVAL RUNES: A re-expanded version of the Younger Futhark to include more sounds. The interest in them is more historical than magickal and is not commonly used for divination.

- RUNES OF HONORIUS: Also known as Theban, they aren't usually used for divination and even though they technically aren't runic, they are still used as sacred scripts.

- WITCH'S RUNES: A modern invention that is used purely for divination; they come in several variations and usually come in thirteen pictograms. Some people find them easy to memorize and are good runes for beginners, because the pictograms are more visually meaningful than the simple lines of the other runic systems, but advanced practitioners can find them useful too.

- **YOUNGER FUTHARK RUNES:** These Scandinavian born runes evolved over time because of the changes throughout history in regards to language use and have fewer characters than most of the others. It is because some of them took on additional sounds meaning that it wasn't necessary anymore to have a full set of characters, which left only sixteen. This makes them a good option to look into if you are struggling to understand and learn the standard Elder Futhark Runes. All you have to do is walk away from the latter and learn it later on.

Now that you have a basic understanding of the twelve rune sets that are of interest to magick practitioners, and before I lay out samples of the Elder Futhark system as promised earlier, there are first some details for us to discuss that will further help your understanding and ultimately your success in using them effectively.

- **RUNE NAME:** Since runes are different across regions and time periods, their names are numerous, so be aware of which system you are using in order to avoid confusion.
- **RUNE NUMBER:** Each rune has a number and knowing the order is important because the order of the runes can help you memorize in a

similar way that you might learn the alphabet. The number is also helpful if you are practicing numerology and even in rune readings where you are trying for a numerical amount such as a calendar date, persons' age or an amount of money.

- SUGGESTED PRONUNCIATION: It is an ancient action to sing the rune names as one cuts the runes, meditates, or even casts spells. There may be different ways to pronounce a rune, so I have suggested simplified breakdowns of each to make it easier.

- SOUNDED OUT: Knowing how it sounds is important if you are going to use or interpret runes as a script as well as for the same reason as above, chanting or singing. It may also be helpful in deciphering someone's name during a reading.

- PICTURING: For beginners, all runes can look alike. Each rune can be seen as something different, and it doesn't necessarily have to be the ones listed here; you can visualize them in any way that helps you to memorize the runes easier.

- INTERPRETATIONS: Each rune governs multiple meanings and in the case of the Elder Futhark at least, the majority of them will have the same beginning sound as the rune that it matches with.

Here is the list of Elder Futhark Runes and a short summary of each category:

FEHU

Rune Number: 1

Suggested Pronunciation: FAY-hoo

Sounded Out: F is 'fee'

Picture: Cow with horns jutting as it looks to the right.

Interpretation: Fertility, fire, fortune

URUZ

Rune Number: 2

Suggested Pronunciation: OO-ROOZ

Sounded Out: U is 'ukulele'

Picture: A wild, horned ox that's now extinct, with its head bowed down.

Interpretation: Useful, utensil

THURISAZ

Rune Number: 3

Suggested Pronunciation: THOOR-ee-sahz

Sounded Out: Th

Picture: A thorn poking from the side of a plant's stem.

Interpretation: Thistle, thorn

ANSUZ

Rune Number: 4

Suggested Pronunciation: AHN-sooz

Sounded Out: Ah

Picture: A magickal staff with blessings of light raining down from it.

Interpretation: Advice, ancestors, authority

RAIDO

Rune Number: 5

Suggested Pronunciation: RYE-thoh

Sounded Out: R

Picture: A capital 'R'

Interpretation: Result, ritual

KEN

Rune Number: 6

Suggested Pronunciation: KEHN

Sounded Out: K

Picture: A stretched out "less than" symbol.

Interpretation: Compassion, comprehension, conclusion

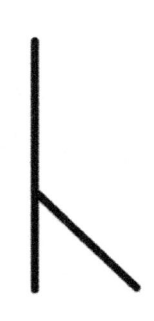

GEBO

Rune Number: 7

Suggested Pronunciation: GIFF-oo

Sounded Out: G like 'gift'

Picture: The top view of a gift bow.

Interpretation: Gift, giving, gratitude

WUNJO

Rune Number: 8

Suggested Pronunciation: WOON-yoh

Sounded Out: W

Picture: A triangle shaped flag that has been planted.

Interpretation: Winning, wonder

HAGALAZ

Rune Number: 9

Suggested Pronunciation: HAH-gah-lahz

Sounded Out: H

Picture: A capital 'H'

Interpretation: Hardship, harm, havoc, hostility

NEID

Rune Number: 10

Suggested Pronunciation: N-EYE-D (rhymes with "vied")

Sounded Out: N like 'need'

Picture: Crossed kindling for a fire.

Interpretation: Necessity, need, neglected

ISA

Rune Number: 11

Suggested Pronunciation: EES

Sounded Out: E like 'sleep'

Picture: A straight, vertical line.

Interpretation: Eternity, inability, intent

JERA

Rune Number: 12

Suggested Pronunciation: YEHR-ah

Sounded Out: There are a couple of interpretations, it could be J like 'journey' or Y like 'year.' This is because Germanic languages often used and still use the letter J to represent a Y sound.

Picture: A winding path.

Interpretation: Journey, joy, yes

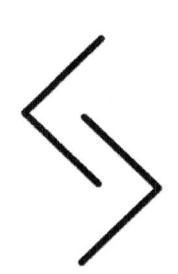

EIHWAZ

Rune Number: 13

Suggested Pronunciation: EYE-wahz

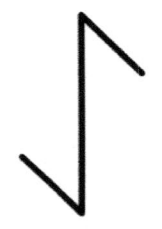

Sounded Out: It's not entirely certain as the vowel has been lost to the past. It might sound like 'eye;' some people do pronounce it as something between E and I.

Picture: A Z that's been reversed and turned on its side.

Interpretation: Adaptability, empowerment, enlightenment

PERTHO

Rune Number: 14

Suggested Pronunciation: PEHR-thoh

Sounded Out: P

Picture: A cauldron with two smokestacks emerging while tipped on the side facing to the right.

Interpretation: Pleasure, poetic, profane

ALGIZ

Rune Number: 15

Suggested Pronunciation: ahl-GHEEZ

Sounded Out: Originally sounded like Z, but some dialects now pronounce it as an R.

Picture: A capital Y with an extra line in between the forks.

Interpretation: Reliability, repel, Zen

SOWILO

Rune Number: 16

Suggested Pronunciation: soh-WEE-loh

Sounded Out: S like 'sun'

Picture: A lightning bolt.

Interpretation: Safety, security, stress

TIWAZ

Rune Number: 17

Suggested Pronunciation: TEE-wahz

Sounded Out: T like 'Tuesday'

Picture: An arrow pointing upward.

Interpretation: Tests, trial, triumph

BERKANAN

Rune Number: 18

Suggested Pronunciation: BEHR-kahn-ahn

Sounded Out: B

Picture: A capital 'B.'

Interpretation: Babies, bear, birth

EHWAZ

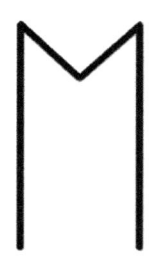

Rune Number: 19

Suggested Pronunciation: AY-wahz

Sounded Out: E like 'expedition'

Picture: A capital 'M.'

Interpretation: Alliance, association, enterprise, expedition

MANNAZ

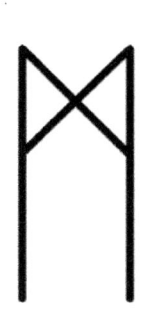

Rune Number: 20

Suggested Pronunciation: MAHN-ahz

Sounded Out: M like "mankind"

Picture: Two parallel lines with an 'x' connecting them at the top

Interpretation: Male, memory, mind, mysticism

LAGUZ

Rune Number: 21

Suggested Pronunciation: LAH-ghooz

Sounded Out: L like 'like'

Picture: An upside down 'L' that's more bent.

Interpretation: Life, love

INGWAZ

Rune Number: 22

Suggested Pronunciation: ING-wahz

Sounded Out: An N or NG like words that end in 'ing'

Picture: A rotated square, like the diamond symbol.

Interpretation: Nourishing, nurturing

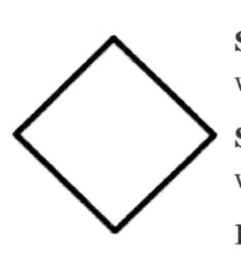

OTHILA

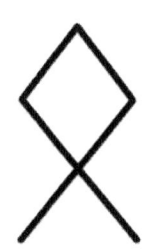

Rune Number: 23

Suggested Pronunciation: OH-thee-LAH

Sounded Out: O like 'home'

Picture: Resembles a cancer ribbon, except with the loop being sharper like a diamond symbol.

Interpretation: Obituaries, origins, owner

DAGAZ

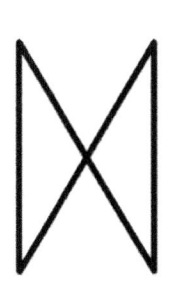

Rune Number: 24

Suggested Pronunciation: DAH-ghaz

Sounded Out: D

Picture: Two D's that are mirroring each other.

Interpretation: Dawn, death, destiny, dusk

There is also an extra rune[3] that is often included in sets to remind the practitioner of the unknown, but it is completely up to you if you wish to include that one. It has no number and thus no sound. It has an interpretation of things that are unknowable, a void, or in the hands of gods.

OGHAM

It's easy for those just starting out to confuse the Ogham alphabet for runes. Both are ancient scripts that were and still are used nowadays for divination, but also magick and writing. Like the Futhark's name coming from the first six letters of its alphabet, Ogham is also named after the first letters of the script and is called *Beith-luis-nin*.

These symbols are an easy alternative if you are carving out symbols on a personal tool and can easily fit into any rune system, as they are made of simple lines that can easily obscure the true meanings of the magick that they are used to conjure up, much like the runes above.

---

[3] The blank rune is the equivalent to the Fool card in a Tarot deck. It can also represent a breath before speaking, the hum of the universe *(the AUM)*, or a total silence that blesses you with the chance to reflect on what you might not know yet. Some believe that it also represents ignorance or a possible sinister destiny if it appears in a reading.

Elemental Symbols

As I mentioned in chapter one, in the practice of witchcraft, depending on one's point of view, there are typically four, sometimes five elements that are connected to different aspects of life. The basic four elements are earth, fire, air, and water. There is a fifth element, the 'spirit' which is also known as the 'aether' or 'ether'. Now, I will go over the symbols that are representative of each with a recap of what each element represents.

Earth

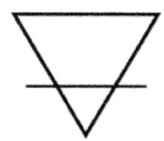

The symbol for earth represents the direction of the north and has strong ties to Mother Earth as well as fertility, sustenance, and wealth. When it is used, it draws the energy from these ideas and aids in growth, life, and enhances nature's work. It resembles a triangle with the top point facing downwards with a horizontal line drawn through the middle.

Fire

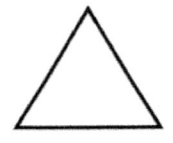

The symbol for fire represents the direction of the south and has strong ties to purification, and new life and beginnings. It is also representative of masculine energy and the destruction that creates new life and opportunities for those who use it in their craft. It resembles a right side up triangle.

Air

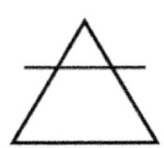

The symbol for air represents the direction of the east and has strong ties to communication and wisdom, as well as the breath and the soul. It is a powerful symbol that invokes greater wisdom and clarity into our lives while also making clearer pathways of insight and communication. It resembles a right side up triangle with a line through the middle.

WATER

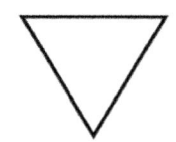

The symbol for water represents the direction of the west and has strong ties to feminine energy as well as the opportunity for healing. Using this symbol invokes the power of banishing negative energy, healing, love, and nurturing. It resembles an upside down triangle.

SPIRIT

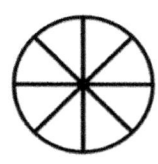

The spirit element represents balance and space, and is considered universal and immaterial. This element connects everything in spirit and represents joy and wellbeing. The symbol represents all directions as well as both feminine and masculine energy. It is commonly used to create the pentacle as the outermost circle, hence why the symbol resembles a circle with four lines drawn in such a way that divides the circle up into eight triangles.

MOON SYMBOLS

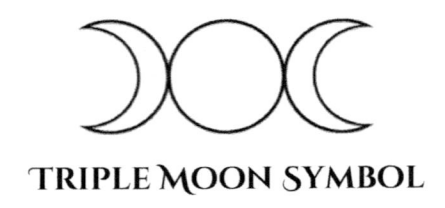

TRIPLE MOON SYMBOL

I mentioned in the introduction the significance of the Triple Moon in connection with the Goddess in Wiccan beliefs, so this symbol should need no introduction of its own. But yes, there is a symbol to invoke the powers that the Triple Moon can bestow upon us when used in rituals.

When this symbol is used, it is a powerful way to draw to us the powers of the moon, and honor womanhood and divine femininity. The way the symbol is drawn represents the phases of the moon as well as the maiden, mother and crone. It resembles the outline of a circle with two crescent moons on each side.

GODDESS SYMBOL

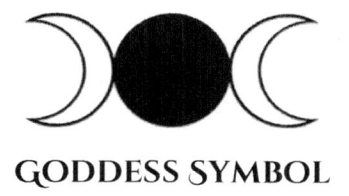

The Goddess symbol is essentially the twin of the Triple Moon as it is exactly the same symbol, with the exception that the full moon is filled in. Compared to the Triple Moon, the Goddess represents the female power in ways that are mysterious and powerful, yet united.

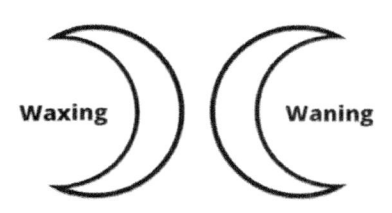

CRESCENT MOON SYMBOL

By itself, the crescent moon represents both of the waning and waxing phases of the moon and is intensely connected to creative power; this particular symbol can be used in specific magick rituals that are tied to these two phases.

Other Symbols

There are many magickal symbols besides runes and the Ogham. There are just too many to list here, and honestly there are some that I can't even try to categorize! I have listed several examples and their meanings that you might find interesting to look through.

Hecate's Wheel Symbol

The Hecate's Wheel symbol is directly associated with the Goddess Hecate and is once again associated with the three phases of the divine femininity of maiden, mother, and crone.

The symbol itself is connected to transformation of women. The symbol resembles a circle with maze-like shapes and a small basic star burst in the middle.

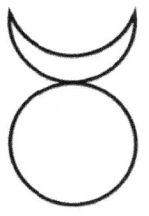

HORNED GOD SYMBOL

This symbol represents the Horned God that I mentioned earlier. It is connected to masculine energy and is the very symbol that invokes the God himself. This symbol is used in fertility rituals and brings about strength and the masculine energy that it is connected with. The symbol resembles a circle with a crescent moon turned on its side to represent the horns.

PENTAGRAM SYMBOL

The Pentagram (a right side up five-pointed star), or the pentacle, as it is called when it is encircled, is more than likely the most well-known symbol of witchcraft, but is also the most controversial. It is representative of the four cardinal directions and the spirit. Ultimately, the pentagram symbolizes unity. It is a powerful symbol to use in your craft as it is filled with the universe's energy, due to containing all the elements that are vital for all life.

SOLAR CROSS SYMBOL

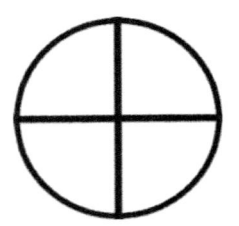

The Solar Cross Symbol is used for rituals that are performed to bring in new beginnings and transformations. The symbol itself is very closely connected with the sun and the four seasons. The symbol can be used to bring attention to these in rituals. It resembles a circle with a horizontal and a vertical line inside, creating a cross.

SPIRAL SYMBOL

The Spiral is commonly felt to be the sign of life and signifies the whole of the cycle of life—from birth, through life, to death, and ultimately to rebirth. The spiral is used to honor life itself and can be found in a very fabric of nature, appearing in the form of something as small as a seashell, to something as colossal as a galaxy.

TRISKELION SYMBOL

This is an ancient Celtic symbol that is believed to represent the Goddess in her three forms of the maiden, mother, and crone. In addition, it is used to represent the land, sea, and sky, and also has a connection to the Goddess Brighid. It resembles a triangle tilted to the right slightly with a spiral emerging from each point.

TRIQUETRA SYMBOL

The Triquetra, also known as the "trinity knot," has an in-depth history in the magick of binding things together. Nowadays, it is often used as another symbol of the Triple Goddess, but is also used to symbolize the interwoven pieces of our existence that are the body, mind, and soul, as well as unity in general. It also represents the earth, wind, and sky in addition to the body, mind, and soul. It resembles a Celtic knot.

Chapter 5

SPELLCASTING AND RITUALS

And we have come now to the chapter that I have no doubt you have been looking forward to since the beginning; we are finally going to cover some spells and rituals! Throughout this chapter, I'll be separating the spells into categories such as love, health, etc. and breaking them down further into whether it is meant for beginner or advanced magick practitioners. But before we begin, let's go over how to get into the correct mindset *before* we cast our magick.

It is important to note that preparation is absolutely crucial up to the point when you perform your magick and it has to be the right kind of preparation; you need to avoid any kind of spontaneity for a couple of reasons. Preparation will help you to gain strength that's needed to perform your magick, as building up your energy is necessary to make the magick happen.

The other reason is that it can protect you from negative energies and block interference from any interruptions.

The best process for preparing for your casting isn't a singular set of steps, but varies for each individual. The goal is still the same—to prepare you to direct your energies to what the spell requires. You can prepare yourself days and even weeks in advance; how much you choose to prepare depends on the limits of your schedule, importance of the spell, and how powerful you want to make it.

Early Stage Preparation

Learn the Spell

Become intimate with the spell which you are about to perform. Whether it is a spell created by others or one that you have discovered yourself, you must memorize the spell and the steps involved; especially if it involves a form of mental direction like chanting.

Timing

I've mentioned the best possible times for certain kinds of spell casting before—how the phases of the moon are a great indicator of when a spell would be at its most potent—however, certain moon phases have other connections as well, such as colors, herbs, animals, runes, chakras, holidays, etc. Certain connections will be brought up later on when we discuss a relevant spell.

I also touched on the fact that the Sabbats and Esbats have their place in magick casting, but the Equinoxes and the Solstices have certain magickal connections of their own—these will also be explained when they are relevant.

However, what I haven't touched on is that there are more sun connections to magickal timings, such as when the sun is in a particular zodiac. Below are the zodiacs with attributes that they connect with the most:

- ARIES: Ambition, optimism, pleasure
- TAURUS: Comfort, pleasure, sensuality
- GEMINI: Balance, community, intelligence
- CANCER: Beginnings, emotions, family, home, support
- LEO: Action, ambition, energy, enlightenment, warmth
- VIRGO: Beginnings, cycles, nurturing, well-being
- LIBRA: Fairness, harmony, romance, unity

- SCORPIO: Changes, darkness, introspection, transformation
- SAGITTARIUS: Consciousness, freedom, optimism, prophecy, unity
- CAPRICORN: Ambition, manifestation, stability
- AQUARIUS: Charity, compassion, hope
- PISCES: Clarity, enchantment, spirituality

I will give more information on the zodiacs in the next chapter. Another connection to the sun that can be utilized for spellcasting are the days of the week as they too have connections to certain spells, such as the following:

- MONDAY: Emotions, home, prophecy
- TUESDAY: Action, assertiveness, energy
- WEDNESDAY: Crossroads, introspection, loss
- THURSDAY: Honor, leadership, loyalty
- FRIDAY: Emotions, pleasure, wisdom
- SATURDAY: Freedom, life, peace
- SUNDAY: Action, ambition, hope

We can also expand upon the days of the week by aligning our spellcasting with the time of day, such as the following:

- DAWN/SUNRISE: Activation, awakening, new beginnings, renewal
- MIDDAY/NOON: Center, light, strength
- SUNSET/DUSK/TWILIGHT: Change, endings, underworld
- MIDNIGHT/DARK NIGHT: Changes, darkness, endings

In connection with the Sabbats and Esbats, each season has their own correlations, as noted below:

- SPRING: Awakening, beginnings, rebirth, renewal
- SUMMER: Growth, light, warmth
- AUTUMN: Abundance, balance, harmony
- WINTER: Darkness, endings, introspection

Now that you have a grasp of how you can time your spells for potency, we'll move on to where you cast your magick.

THE SACRED SPACE

Your sacred space is the area you have dedicated to castings spells and rituals, and is also used for meditation and worship. Your sacred space is where you would put your altar. You can dedicate a permanent or temporary spot in your home or outside for this.

One of the necessities to creating your sacred space is to mark out the barrier that surrounds it. There are various ways to mark the barrier; it's quite common to use chalk or draw in the dirt if outside or use a rug if inside. Your barrier should be a circle and all that is within the circle becomes your sacred space.

CLEANING AND CLEANSING THE SPACE

Once you have chosen your sacred space, it must be thoroughly cleaned. Start by sweeping the area with a broom to clear away any dirt and dust; if outside you should sweep away any loose dirt and debris to clear your circle. After you have done this, cleanse your space to take away negative or unwanted energies and influences.

You do this by taking the broom and 'sweeping' the air by starting on the ground and sweeping as high as you can reach. At the same time, you must be consciously sweeping away all the negativity by starting in the east and sweeping the space counter clockwise.

You can also cleanse the area by 'smudging,' during which you take a lit bundle or stick of sage, or sage incense, and use the smoke to cleanse the space. After you light it, again you start in the east and walk counter clockwise through the space while making sure that the smoke reaches the whole area.

If you're cleansing a space for the first time, sprinkle some salt around the area and ring a bell three times; once the last chime has faded, picture your space cleansed from all negativity.

DEDICATING THE SPACE

After your space has been cleansed, it's time to dedicate it. There are various ways to do this, but as it's your space it's up to you to decide what's best for you. Here is one of the most common ways of dedicating your space for you to try, which is to tell the spirit out loud that you are dedicating the space and you anoint the corners of your space using oils of Frankincense and Myrrh. There is also a dedication ritual that can be done, especially if your space is a temporary one:

Easy Sacred Space Dedication Ritual

You Need

- One white candle
- Frankincense oil
- Myrrh oil

Instructions

1. Anoint the candle with the oils before lighting it, then hold it in your hands. Start from the west and walk around your space clockwise while letting the candle burn out inside your space.

2. Additional ways to dedicate your space is by choosing items that have personal meaning to you. If you don't have an altar in your space, you can place decorations, like your favorite crystals or stones at each of the cardinal directions, or display pictures of your favorite deities to bring their energy into your space.

PROTECTING THE SPACE

Once you dedicate your space, you now have to protect it from anything that is negative and intrusive. You can use mirrors, which reflect positive and negative energy. There are also symbols such as a pentagram or the Algiz rune which work well. You can keep protective crystals and stones such as Agate, Beryl, Emerald, Jasper, and Zircon (among others) within your space to help support the protection. Another simple but effective option is to either hang or lay some dried basil around your space or to just sprinkle some sea salt around.

Spell Preparations

PERSONAL

In the days leading up to the time you cast your spell or perform a ritual, there are a couple of things that need to be done to prepare yourself to be in the right form to make your magick.

Ritual Bathing

It is considered rude to the gods, as well as to the other people in your circle, to enter it without having cleaned yourself beforehand; however, hygiene isn't the only reason to take ritual baths. It is acceptable to take baths/showers up until your big day/night, as cleaning yourself can help your skin slough off any unwanted moods or energies before entering the circle as well as helping with the intent.

Despite the heading above, it doesn't specifically have to be an actual bath, it can be a shower or even cleaning off with a bucket of water! What makes it a ritual is what you do to make it special. You could do something simple, like adding salt to your bath water, or pouring some salt water over your head if showering.

You can also add things like bath salts, oils, and soap to the water that might be connected in some way to your magickal intentions, such as rose for love. Please make sure before adding anything that it is safe to do so to avoid allergies or any irritation.

You don't even necessarily have to add anything to the water itself, you could just read a book or put on some relaxing music, anything that adds to a positive mood for your upcoming casting.

Other Preparations

But it isn't just bathing that helps with your preparations, there are other things you can do like make your favorite dinner, or anything really that can put you in a positive mood. Also, when you're going to bed, you should run through the spell's instructions in your head and visualize the intended result, if you live with other people then request that they don't disturb you while sleeping or mentally preparing; you also need to get at least a total eight hours of sleep on the night before you cast because lack of sleep takes away the vital energy that you need to cast successfully and even after you have woken up the next morning, try not to move or talk for at least fifteen minutes, just focus on the spell itself and don't let your mind wander.

There is also a matter of what you can wear for your ritual, and the answer is whatever makes you feel comfortable. You could wear shoes or go barefoot, have special robe(s) or kimonos, or if you are comfortable doing so, you could always do what is referred to as "going skyclad," which means being only clothed by the sky[4].

Preparing Your Tools

You should also make sure that all of your tools, materials, and ingredients are all ready to go. If you are a true beginner, you may not know how to fully cleanse your tools yet. If this is the case don't worry, I will explain how in a moment. It's worth noting that it's more than just removing physical impurities, you will also need to cleanse them in between magick workings so as to remove any residual energy; these

---

[4] Ritual nudity is usually referred to as "skyclad" in both Wicca and Modern Paganism. It is based on the belief that physically the body is the origin of a lot of the energy used in Wiccan rituals, meaning that if you perform a ritual skyclad, you can maximize the radiant energy that you release.

same rules also apply to crystals and other items. You need to be sure that they are all properly cleansed before you charge them for your goals and intentions.

Here are a few different cleansing methods that you can use to consecrate your tools; however, like all things there are upsides and downsides to each, so choose wisely:

CRYSTAL CLEANSING

While crystals themselves need cleansing, some crystals like clear and smoky quartz, as well as citrine, actually don't hold onto energy, so they are referred to as "self-cleansing" crystals. These self-cleansing crystals can be used to clean crystals that do hold onto energy. Simply place the crystal you would like to clean into or onto a cluster of self-cleansers and leave them for 24 hours.

EARTH OR SALT CLEANSING

You can cleanse an object by burying it in soil or salt for a good 12-24 hours to remove unwanted energies. However, salt can damage certain items and it also could be easy to lose an item in the soil, so you can get around this by using a container such as a bowl or a pot and your item would still benefit from this method of cleansing.

MOONLIGHT & SUNLIGHT CLEANSING

Both moonlight and sunlight can cleanse and even charge objects, depending on your intentions. Please take into account that when using this method you should keep track of the moon phase and current season because they can affect the resulting energy that your items absorb.

SMOKE CLEANSING

This technique uses herb smoke to cleanse an object, a room, or even yourself. The go-to herb is sage, but other herbs that can be used are cedar and rosemary. But as I mentioned above with the smudging, it isn't just herb bundles that can be used to cleanse, you can also use incense smoke.

Smoke cleansing is simple, just light your incense or herb bundle, blow out any flames that are smoldering and let the smoke waft over the object, your body, or around the room. This allows the smoke to break up the energies that are stuck or unwanted and transform them back into the neutral and free-flowing energy that you need.

However, something you have to consider before you choose smoke cleansing is if you have any pets, and the health of those pets that you do have. Cats and dogs might be okay if they aren't close to the smoke and the room is well ventilated, but you should never expose smaller pets to smoke as their lungs are very small and can have bad health from even the smallest amount of smoke.

There is also your own health to take into consideration. If you suffer from asthma or some form of lung and/or breathing disorder, then this method is quite dangerous and you should consider the alternatives in this list.

SOUND CLEANSING

Instruments like bells, drums, tambourines, and rainmakers are all used to remove unwanted energies. This method is good for large spaces and can even be combined with dancing to add additional energy. Naturally this should only be performed if you are alone or are living with people who wouldn't mind the noise.

WATER CLEANSING

Water cleansing can be done in a variety of ways; you can bathe, wash, or even let your tools soak to remove unwanted energies. You can also fill up a spray bottle with your charged water and use it to mist a room.

Water is one of the most powerful methods of personal cleansing. Putting yourself in a good, cleansing bath doesn't just remove unwanted energies, it can also take away curses, emotional issues, and bad spells and spirits. Water is a multi-tool for cleansing.

You need to be careful that water isn't going to damage the object that you are trying to cleanse, or that you won't be harmed by the water when you come into contact with it. Some crystals, herbs and stones can actually be destroyed by water, or they can become toxic once they have touched water, so research carefully.

One more thing to remember about cleansing your sacred objects is that regardless of what method you choose, the act of cleansing will not drive the magick alone. It is by adding your focused intention behind the cleansing that this will happen.

For most of the methods to work, you have to feel the intention of returning the items to a state where the energy is neutral. There are a few ways to do this—by visualizing that the energy is changing, picturing how the changing energy will feel or just holding the idea in your head. As long as you hold onto that intention, the magick will do the rest.

Final Preparations

Before you actually cast a spell or a ritual, you have to clear your mind of everything except your desire to perform your magick and the image of your magick taking effect. Personally, I use yoga and meditative exercises to clear unnecessary thoughts from my mind. Another method to enter a mental state that will help boost your magick is to set the atmosphere beforehand with some calming music. You can also burn incense or a candle, or you can use a combination of any of the things that I have mentioned to help your process.

In the cases where you are performing magick that involves multiple people working together, the group should prepare by involving themselves in an activity that helps to harmonize them, such as playing a game, singing the same song, or even putting on the same oil or perfume, anything that can align the energy of all the participants.

Remember your safeguards, both physical and spiritual. Ensuring that these are in place will help your magick go smoothly. For the physical, if you live with others who aren't participating, ideally perform when they aren't at home. If that's not possible, kindly ask them to help you out by not disturbing you and to keep noise levels down; if you live alone it is also important to keep distractions to a minimum. Turn off the TV and cell phone. Reduce any unnecessary background noise where you can. The only sounds in the air should be the music you have chosen to enhance your mental focus.

As for the spiritual safeguards, you should put on completely different clothing from what you had been wearing before, as those clothes may have built up negative energy that would interfere with your spell work. If you have a particular robe or set of clothing that you wear specifically for your spell work, then put those on.

Another way to help protect yourself against psychic attacks during your performance is by anointing your forehead and your heart area with sandalwood oil. You can also contemplate using a pinch of regular or sea salt in each corner of the room to protect you.

One last piece of advice to help protect against negative forces is to visualize a powerful white light. Imagine this white light filling the space you're in and surrounding your circle. Picture yourself bathing in this light, then have the light hover over you as it protects you. Having the light around you works just as well as the salt and oil. If you are performing magick that might be potentially dangerous or tricky, it is a great idea to do all three of these protection methods. It also helps to picture the white light either filling the room or surrounding your sacred circle.

Back in chapter two, I mentioned centering, grounding and shielding. Before you begin your spell work, I'm going to give you some more detail and some techniques to use.

Centering is essentially learning how to connect with your energy work, so centering is something that you should be learning to master before you actually learn about any spellcasting. As mentioned before, each magickal tradition has a different point of view on what centering is and how it's done, but here's a simple exercise that can work for you:

1. Start off by finding a place where you can work undisturbed, just like with spell and ritual work, and have no distractions. Find yourself a place to sit as this is best done while seated as you could fall asleep lying down or fall over if standing up. Once you're seated, take a deep breath and exhale, do this a few times until you're breathing even and regularly, once you do this, then you can start visualizing energy.

2. Rub your palms lightly together like you're trying to warm them up, then move them an inch or two apart. You should be feeling a charge—a tingling between your palms—that's energy! Don't be concerned if you don't feel it right away, just try again. After a while you'll start to notice that the space between your

palms feels different, like you're feeling a resistance if you try to carefully push them together.

3. Every time you need to center, you must always follow the steps of regulating your breathing and focusing your energy. After you have mastered this and can tell what energy feels like, you can actually play with it by focusing on the area of resistance. You can start simple like picturing the energy expanding and contracting like a balloon, or even visualize it expanding to where it surrounds your entire body.

4. After a while, it becomes second nature to you and that will be helpful as you are developing a foundation for the energy work needed for many magickal traditions. Centering is important because when we perform our magick, we never use our personal energy for rituals, we draw it from the earth. Centering helps to do exactly that, center the energy for usage.

Now when it comes to grounding, I mentioned that it is a crucial technique used to dispel the excess energy that we may possibly build up from our casting, but it is also used to expel any negative energy that we might build up for various other reasons, such as from having an argument; grounding is meant to put energy into the earth or an object that is not needed. But grounding isn't necessarily just done after completing a performance, some witches even 'ground' themselves before they cast any magick in order to throw away any unwanted energy or vibes that they might have built up from the day, such as a stressful work day or an incident of road rage.

Here are a few grounding techniques:

- BREATHING DEEPLY AND SLOWLY—Picture pushing the excess energy out of your body each time you exhale. Slow and controlled breathing is key to reducing unwanted energy.

- RUNNING WATER—Just sitting by or getting into running water is great for grounding. You can go swimming or just stand in the shower and picture excess energy running away from you with the water.

- SHAKING HANDS—Not with someone else, but picturing the energy being pushed into your hands and shaking it off the way you would shake off water. Be sure that you don't direct this excess energy at others as they may end up absorbing it.

- STONES—Black stones like jet and obsidian have the ability to absorb excess energy, so they are great stones to ground in a pinch if needed. Carry a small one in your pocket if you are outside or keep a large hunk at home; pour the extra energy into your hands like the shaking hands.

- TREE GROUNDING—Similar to shaking hands and using stones, you picture the extra energy going into your hands, then you touch the trunk of a tree and think of the energy flowing from your hands into the trunk, then down then trunk through the roots and into the earth.

Now for shielding, it is important to familiarize yourself with this before starting any advanced energy work. It works by creating an energy shield around you to control what energies you pick up and what you give off.

Shielding is great if you are trying to improve your psychic skills by increasing your sensitivity to the environment. It also helps filter out excess 'noise' like picking up the vibrations of anyone around you. With a little practice, you'll find it pretty easy to create a shield.

1. Firstly, think of a protective image that you can use to surround yourself with, like a bubble, a ring of fire, a suit of armor, or anything suitable that your imagination can clearly visualize.

2. Once you have chosen an image, find a place to sit comfortably, relax and ground by taking several deep breaths. Picture a ball of energy at the base of your spine, make it a color that you associate with protection, and focus until you can clearly sense it.

3. Now expand your energy ball until it surrounds your body, taking the shape of your chosen image. Make your mental image strong enough to deflect unwanted energies from its surface. Now stand up and move around. Your shield should remain in place and move with you.

4. Try to practice this technique daily until you can bring your shield up at will. Once you've mastered this, you must practice taking it back down again. Visualize your shield's energy being sucked back into a ball at the base of your spine and ground the excess energy.

You now have the basics of energy work down. Well done for making it this far! Any new knowledge or understanding you have taken on has already helped your power grow. Now it's time to cast your circle!

Casting the Circle

As I mentioned earlier, you mark out your circle in your sacred space either physically with chalk, or with your energy if necessary. It can be as big or small as you need for its purpose. A circle is absolutely crucial if you are performing powerful magick such as calling upon a god.

When you cast the circle, you do it after you've cleansed and purified your space. You can draw it using just your fingers, but you may choose to use an athame or a wand. It is recommended that you learn without tools before beginning to utilize them because it is handier this way in case of an emergency.

1. To cast your circle, you must first choose which direction to begin from. Witches can use any of the cardinal directions, but most tend to start either in the east (where the sun rises), or to the north (the direction connected to the earth).

2. Next you ground yourself and then visualize yourself drawing energy up from the earth into yourself. Extend the index and middle fingers

on your preferred hand and picture the energy flowing into those fingers.

3. Walk clockwise around the circle and picture the energy flowing through you. Move slowly, focus, and breathe deeply.

4. Once you have walked your circle and arrive back at the starting point, stop. Now visualize the boundary in your mind; once you see it, extend it above your head and below the ground so that it surrounds you. Hold it in your mind for a moment to increase its power.

Now that you have cast your circle, it's time for some spells!

SPELLS

GLAMOR

Glamor spells are basically magickal veils that bring out one's natural beauty while masking everything else. Despite being used for centuries, glamor spells aren't very widely known. When you're casting a glamor spell, you either choose the aspects that you want to enhance, or visualize beauty and allow the spell to choose for you. A glamor spell will usually only last a day or so.

You'll find this first spell easy. It only requires two items, some focus, and a bit of planning.

Physical Beauty Glamor Spell

You Need

- A mirror
- A bowl of rose water, made with either rose oil or rose petals

> **Special Considerations:** This is ideally performed during a full moon, but it can be effective during other phases, so long as there is some moon power (so not during a new moon).

Instructions

1. Leave the bowl of rose water under the moonlight through the entire night.
2. During the next day, sit in front of the mirror with the water. Put your hands over the water with your palms facing the bowl.
3. Close your eyes and picture the highest version of yourself, don't go too drastic, just start off small so you can see the changes.
4. Once that picture is solid in your mind, describe this ideal image to the water and send the energy out using your hands. Describe yourself three times.

5. Take as much time as you need to send out your energy. When you're ready, wash your face and hands with the water. For the best results, do this every day until you see strong changes.

This next spell is a different type of glamor, one that will help you to "fly under the radar" and is good if you don't want to be noticed. You don't need any items, but this is a spell that you need to practice in order for it to succeed and has a few considerations.

Invisibility Glamor

Special Considerations: It won't be as effective if someone is looking for you or if you're making a lot of noise while casting.

Before attempting this spell, dress to blend in. Dress professionally at the office, or wear casual clothes if on a college campus. You want to make it easy for people to overlook you.

It's best that you start practicing at home and around people you know before trying this in public.

Instructions

1. Start by going somewhere secluded where you can focus. You're going to be tapping into a

signature or energy, and then maintain it for as long as you can.

2. Sit comfortably and close your eyes, feel the surface of your body, where your skin meets your clothes or the air around you, and turn it into a more tangible part of yourself.

3. When you're ready, picture the barrier between yourself and the rest of the world disappearing, leaving your outline hazy and indistinct. Imagine that your body is like mist, that someone can look right through you if they tried. Work on making this signature strong and cement it in your mind.

4. Once you're feeling comfortable, try opening your eyes and getting up and walking around. Try not to catch sight of your reflection as that can pull you from your headspace. Are you imagining this sense of intangibility while you're moving?

5. When you are able to keep up the feeling, then you can try it with another person around. Keep practicing and try this around different people and situations as you get more comfortable.

Health and Healing

In such a chaotic world, it can sometimes feel difficult to maintain our health, so this section provides various approaches to increase your reserves of positive energy while decreasing stress. Remember that these spells are not a replacement for any medical treatment; always seek help from a medical professional if needed! The following spell is a simple one that only requires two items and is good for those of us who enjoy using crystals and stones.

Red Jasper for Energy and Endurance

You Need

- One medium-sized red jasper, polished
- A journal or writing paper

Instructions

1. Clear and charge your stone before using it and pick a day to begin.
2. From the day that you start, keep the jasper on your person for seven straight days. Take it out of your pocket/purse several times a day to hold it in your hand.
3. At the end of each day, write down any emotional, physical, or psychic impressions that you've noticed, no matter how subtle.

4. As an extra step, you can try this spell again with a different stone and compare the results!

Some people thrive on being busy, but most magickal types like us don't; if you've got a busy day or week coming up that you're dreading, here's a relaxing spell that you can even turn into a ritual.

Busy Bee Balancing Talisman

You Need

- A cup of chamomile tea, preferably sweetened with honey
- One white candle
- A piece of amethyst, jade, rose quartz, or other calming stone
- **Optional:** Incense, either lavender or another calming scent

Instructions

1. If you decide to use the incense, this is the time to light it up. Now brew the tea.
2. As the tea steeps, light the candle and gaze at the flame for a few moments.

3. Take a few sips of tea and several deep breaths. Put the stone in your dominant hand, placing the palm of your other hand on top to charge the stone with calm and peaceful energy.

4. Say these words, "I have infinite time, in my sacred space, with peace and calm to go at my pace. I bring this calm to the day(s) ahead, peacefully moving wherever I'm led."

5. Pass the stone over the candle flame three times.

6. It is now charged to help you during your busy times, carry it around with you and hold it whenever you feel the need.

HOME PROTECTION AND PURIFICATION

Our homes are where we are meant to feel safe and yet they are also vulnerable to attacks, both physical and metaphysical. This section gives you the tools to protect your home and purify it in the case of an attack.

This spell is a little tricky as it involves putting together a magick bottle containing a fair few items.

Home Protection Witch Bottle / Spell Jar

You Need

- One empty glass bottle with a cork
- A quarter cup of sea salt or soil, with the best results being soil from your own yard
- At least one protective crystal. (black tourmaline, obsidian, onyx, or smoky quartz)
- Three crushed cloves of garlic
- A pinch of rose thorns or stinging nettles
- Three bay leaves
- At least three nails, sewing needles, or other sharp, metal objects
- A tablespoon of one or more protective herbs. (basil, dill, fennel, juniper, rosemary, tarragon)
- Some vinegar, any kind
- One black candle
- **Optional:** Dried sage, either loose leaf or a smudge stick

> **Special Considerations:** The sharp objects require careful handling, so gloves are recommended to protect yourself.
>
> To make this spell its most effective, once it has been cast, the bottle should be hidden or buried. You can leave it out in the open if you really want to but it may affect its power.
>
> You can personalize the bottle however you want, but you need to include at least one thing from each category: crystals, herbs, and sharp metal objects.

INSTRUCTIONS

1. If you decide to use the dried sage, use it to cleanse your altar or workspace before constructing the bottle.

2. When you are ready to start, light the black candle and say the following words: "Protective spirits, attend my work and add your power to mine. As I create this magick for my home, grant me your protection divine."

3. Now add your salt or soil, putting enough to cover the bottom of the bottle, then add the crystal, the garlic, and the nettles/thorns.

4. Give the bottle a careful shake and then add the bay leaves, sharp metal, and the rest of the herbs.

5. Pour the vinegar in until the bottle is full, but leave enough space for the cork to go in. Cork the bottle and give it another shake as you say the following words: "Protective spirits, honor my work and add your power to mine. Now the power within this bottle grants my home protection divine. It is done."

6. Seal off your work by holding the candle over the bottles' top until a few drops of melted wax have landed on the cork.

7. Hide the bottle somewhere near your home's entrance.

LOVE

Love is one of the most common reasons that people may turn to magick; however, while this section contains some spells that can help to attract a potential new love interest or a new friendship, I am only willing to use and share spells that help to attract in a positive manner and do not condone any kind of magickal actions that interfere with a person's free will.

I'll start off with a simple spell that helps attract new friendships.

Spell for New Friendships

You Need

- One small crystal. (Carnelian, clear quartz, lapis lazuli, or rose quartz)
- One yellow spell or votive candle
- Lavender Essential Oil

> **Special Considerations:** This spell is best performed when the moon is waxing, but if you have an upcoming social encounter during a waning moon, then don't let that stop you!

Instructions

1. Use the lavender oil to anoint the candle.
2. Put the stone in your dominant hand with your palm facing up and lay your other palm on top.
3. Hold your hands together, close your eyes and visualize yourself being surrounded by positive people that you feel good being around.
4. When you've grasped onto that feeling, take a deep breath and exhale. Open your eyes.
5. Put the stone in front of the candle, light the candle as you say these words: "Friendships new and true, let our kindred souls unite."

6. Carry the stone with you when leaving your home and keep it where you can see it when you are home.

This next spell is for attracting new love or renewing it in an existing relationship. I've kept it simple for those who are new to herb work.

Three-Herb Love Charm

You Need

- Dried Basil
- Dried Hibiscus
- Dried Lavender
- One small rose quartz crystal
- A small square of soft cloth (preferably silk or velvet) in pink, red, violet, or white
- A length of pink, red, violet, or white ribbon

Instructions

1. Hold the rose quartz in your hands and charge it with loving vibrations by meditating on how you want to feel when your goal has come to life.

2. Lay the cloth out and carefully put the crystal on it.

3. Sprinkle a pinch of each of the herbs on the crystal. As you do so, name each herb and confirm its purpose, like: "With this (herb name) I manifest love in my life."

4. Fold the cloth over the crystal and wrap it carefully until you can tie the ribbon around it.

5. Carry the charm with you and/or put it under your pillow at night.

SUCCESS

The need to succeed is the second most frequent desire behind wanting to work with magick, but it is a delicate motive as you don't want to just take success away from someone else. Instead, what you want to do is attract success from unlikely places and these spells for prosperity are here to help you do just that.

This first spell is an easy one with few items and steps. It is powerful in the way it helps you to nail one thing that we always dread in the working world: the job interview.

Job Interview Success Spell

You Need

- One orange or gold candle
- Incense (Cinnamon, frankincense or lilac)
- Pen or pencil, and a piece of paper
- One small piece of citrine, lapis lazuli, or tiger's eye

> **Special Considerations:** This spell works best when the moon is waxing but don't be afraid to use it if you have a job interview when the moon is waning.

Instructions

1. Light the incense and anoint the candle with the oil.
2. Take a few moments to visualize yourself feeling calm and confident at your interview.
3. On the paper, write down three reasons why you are the best candidate for the position.
4. Fold the paper into a triangle that is only a few inches big and put it in front of the candle.
5. Light the candle and say the following words: "In perfect place and perfect time, as I light this candle, the job is mine."

6. Quickly pass the crystal through the candle flame and put it on top of the paper.
7. Leave the candle to burn out safely on its own.
8. Bring the folded paper and crystal with you to the interview.
9. Once you've gotten the job, tear the paper into small pieces and recycle it, congratulate yourself, but don't forget to thank the powers that be!

This next spell is a little tricky as one of the items needed is an oil that is most powerful if you make it yourself but shouldn't be attempted by a witch who is at the very beginning of their practice.

Calling in the Cash

You Need

- One gold spell or votive candle
- Wealth Attraction Oil (recipe after spell)
- A one, five, ten, or twenty dollar bill (or higher if you are comfortable carrying it around with you)
- One green or gold ribbon

> **Special Considerations:** If you are having trouble getting a gold candle then you can substitute with a green candle, but you should supplement the spell by having gold objects around your space like pyrite or gold coins or jewelry if this happens.
>
> For the paper bill, you want to use as high a denomination as possible because it "raises the bar" on what you call in, but don't be discouraged if you only have smaller bills, you can always re-do the spell using a bigger bill at a later time.
>
> Being an abundance spell, this is best done when the moon is waxing.

Instructions

1. Before you start, anoint your temples, third eye, and pulse points with the oil, then anoint the candle starting from the base up to the top.

2. Anoint the bill at each corner on both sides, then fold the bill into a triangle and bind with the ribbon.

3. Light the candle and tilt it over the center of the folded bill so that a little bit of wax drips onto the ribbon.

4. Put the candle in its holder and when the wax on the bill has dried a little, put the bill gently between your palms.

5. Say the following words three times: "Essence of abundance, I call you forth into my life in the form of solid currency."
6. Leave the candle to burn out on its own, carry the bill with you for at least a month.

Wealth Attraction Oil Recipe

You Need

- A quarter cup of carrier oil (Almond, grape seed, jojoba, olive, or sunflower oil)
- A small dropper bottle
- A vial of each essential oil below
- Three drops of bergamot
- One drop of basil
- One drop of patchouli
- One drop of sandalwood

Instructions

1. Never, ever forget about the carrier oil! Essential oils on their own are strong and can cause damage to your skin, carrier oils allow them to be used on the skin safely!

2. While creating the blend, charge it while visualizing your intentions. You can help enhance the energy of the finished product by playing elevating music. Once you've put the cap on your new blend, hold the bottle between your palms and send your magickal power into it.

3. Always use the oil in the way that the spell directs you to—to anoint candles and tools. Store it in a cool, dark place and try to use the whole bottle within a year.

Taking Down the Circle

Now that you know the kind of spells you can cast, it's time to learn how to take down your circle. Start at the same point you did when you cast your circle and move around it counterclockwise. This time, as you draw the circle with your index and middle fingers (as you did before) visualize returning the energy to the earth, do not keep the energy in your body! When you are finished, ground again.

Is the Magick Working?

That's a tricky question to answer as every spell is different, as well as the person who cast it. What may be an obvious sign to one witch may not be so obvious to another. However, there are five signs that most people tend to experience after they have cast a successful spell.

MOOD CHANGES

The first and most common sign that a spell has been successful are feelings of clarity and happiness right after casting, usually coming from the satisfaction and confidence of knowing that you cast the right spell at the right time, and that's always a good sign. These feelings can appear the moment you have finished and can last for days or even weeks afterward.

If you aren't feeling different, don't worry, just stay positive and have faith that your spell will work anyway.

SIGNS AND OMENS FROM NATURE

Take a look around. When a spell is working, the universe will send all sorts of signs, you just have to find them. Some signs come in the forms of weather changes, trees, birds, and even cloud formations. Clear your mind and go for a walk. Signs are different for everyone and will speak to you on a personal level, in ways that only you will understand.

DREAM MESSAGES

While all dreams have a meaning, after you've cast a spell you should pay particular attention to the dreams that you have, especially the emotions that they invoke in you; if the emotions are positive then they could be a sign of manifestation. However, if they are negative, then you need to calm yourself and try to analyze the meanings, those could just be a result of something in your subconscious that needs to be resolved.

COINCIDENCES

Believe it or not, coincidences are actually another pretty common sign that a spell is working! Whether it is meeting someone new or talking to someone you haven't spoken to in a long time, or another thing entirely, a coincidence can be a sign that your spell is working effectively. The more you recognize the coincidences, the more messages you're receiving.

REAL LIFE INTERACTIONS

Naturally, the best signs of a spell working are the results themselves! Cast a spell for more money and you get a call about a promotion or higher paying job? Then congratulations, you're becoming a powerful witch! If something unexpected happens in your life, be confident that your desires have been heard and granted!

However, the spells in this chapter are only a small pool of what we are capable of when we tap into our magick, in the next chapter we will take a look at the more serious sides of spellcasting.

CHAPTER 6

BANISHING, MANIFESTING, PROTECTING

The three types of spells we are covering in this chapter are some serious magick—not that all magick isn't serious—but some magick just requires a little more from a witch. We will be going over a set of 'active' spells. Unlike the more passive spells where you have to wait for something to come to you (like love or money), you will actively be bringing something toward you or pushing forces away.

BANISHING

Banishing spells are used to get rid of energy, forces, or even people that we don't want around us. Please be aware that in some traditions this kind of magick can be seen as a kind of manipulation that infringes on the free will of another and therefore may be frowned upon, but if it's something that you wish to explore and have nothing against it, then there is nothing stopping you from doing a little magick to help do away with life's annoyances.

There are a variety of ways that you can banish someone, this first one is a simple one with only a few steps and a couple of items.

LEAVE ME ALONE SPELL

You Need

- A piece of paper and something to write with
- A black candle

Instructions

1. Write the name of the person that you want to stop bothering you on the paper.
2. Light the candle and use it to burn the paper, but only around the edges. As you burn the paper, announce that you are burning away whatever negative feelings they may have toward you.
3. Burn as much of the paper as you can, until all that is left is their name.
4. Take this bit of paper and bring it to the place where you normally see the person, whether it is school, work, etc. and dig a hole and bury the

paper there. You can also tear up this last bit of paper into tiny pieces and allow it to blow and scatter into the winds.

But what if you are wanting to get rid of someone that's a little less...solid? Some magickal practitioners choose to spend their time communicating with the dead, which is a touchy subject that I won't be covering in this book. What I will say is that sometimes there could be an unwanted presence attached to the practitioner and they might not wish to leave.

It's also worth saying that if you decide to do any kind of spirit work, you definitely need to cleanse your area first by smudging, circle casting, or even praying. Or maybe you are just unlucky enough to move into a house that's haunted and would like the unwanted guest to leave, then there are a few ways to go about it depending on the spirits' behavior.

Getting Rid of an Unwanted Spirit

You Need

- Your voice
- Items that help to cleanse, purify and/or smudge (some cases)
- Psychically gifted people to help (during certain circumstances)

Instructions

1. The first and simplest way to get rid of an unwanted spirit is just to tell it to leave. You need to be blunt and firm, focus to feel the presence and say the words "this isn't the place for you, and it's time for you to leave." Then offer the spirit the blessing "I wish you happiness in your new place." More often than not, this is enough to solve this kind of problem.

2. But, if the spirit happens to be a stubborn one, then you may need to be more aggressive. In this case, you may want to create your own cleansing ritual by incorporating smudging and/or purification techniques and being more assertive toward the spirits such as ordering them to leave rather than asking them to leave.

3. And then, there are the cases where your spirit could be outright hostile and being firm isn't enough. In cases like these, you would have to cleanse, smudge, and banish. You have to be extremely assertive in a case like this, so if you have to shout out that the spirit isn't welcome, then do it! If all else fails, you may have to get assistance from some psychically gifted individuals to help you.

Since you now have an idea about how to force negativity out of your life, we shall discuss how to receive what you desire.

Manifesting

Unlike the spells from the previous chapter which are geared toward specific desires, manifestation magick isn't used for a single category but rather for any strong desire that you want to bring to life. Manifestation spells are among some of the most powerful there are and require a very clear articulation in regards to your wish, whether it is written down or shouted out.

Firstly we shall start with a basic but very powerful manifestation spell that includes affirmations and some sigil work.

WRITING OUT YOUR MANIFESTATION

YOU NEED

- One to three pieces of paper and something to write with
- A wish box[5]

Special Considerations: I am going to give you the basic spell which you should modify in regards to how you feel and what you want to manifest.

INSTRUCTIONS

1. Think about what you want and write it down in as much detail as possible. Continue to focus on what you want, picture it in your mind. Imagine it happening. Imagine how you feel as if it was happening at that moment.

2. Write down your affirmation, such as how I once affirmed how the Universe knew how to connect me with a car, and that it revealed the next steps to discovering the car I needed, and

---

[5] A wish box (also referred to as a manifestation / intention / creation box) is a sacred storage space for the goals and dreams you want to manifest. It strengthens your connection with the universe transmitting your intentions and attracting your desires.

that I was grateful that the path to the car had been quick and easy. You can use a second piece of paper to draw out your desire.

3. You should create a sigil now. It is not necessary if you really don't want to, but a sigil can help you to get results quicker. First, take what you wrote out in step one and break it down to a single sentence. Say that you want a house, you can write it as if it has already happened: "I live in the best home that suits my wants and needs." Then you refine it further by changing it, such as taking out all the vowels or all the consonants. Then take the remaining letters and create your sigil by intertwining them or making them into shapes. You can use a second (or third) piece of paper to practice and figure out your final sigil. Once you're happy with your sigil, then draw it on the back of your affirmation paper.

4. Put your affirmation paper in a wish box. If you want to add a little more power to your desire then you can put a crystal that corresponds with your desire in the box as well.

5. Take your paper out daily and read your affirmation, it will help you connect with your desire. You can also take it out and meditate on it just before bedtime by thinking about your wish coming true and how it will look and feel.

6. Once your wish has come true, you burn your affirmation paper outside and scatter the ashes in the dirt.

Sometimes just writing down your affirmation may not be enough. You can add more power to your manifestation spells by adding a few more items and steps, such as adding crystals, herbs, or cleansing.

MANIFESTING EXACTLY WHAT YOU WANT

You Need

- One or more things to represent the four elements
- Ingredients meaningful to your wish
- **Optional:** piece of paper

Instructions

1. Time your spell according to your specific desire via the moon phase, day of the week, etc.
2. Cleanse your space.
3. Have the appropriate ingredients that correspond to the four elements and your desire in your cleansed space. There are few

limits as to what you can have in regards to herbs, crystals, and even colors, as long as they connect to the elements and/or your wish.

4. Articulate your intentions, whether it is written down or said aloud. You can create a poem, a mantra, or use simple language to articulate your intentions. Always use positive words; never use words like 'can't,' 'no,' 'won't,' etc.

5. Ask for help from a higher power, whether it is from gods, spirits, or the universe.

6. When your spell comes true, do not forget to say thank you; acknowledging the source of your wish coming true with gratitude will make the source more willing to help you in the future.

Manifestation can be a wonderful way to bring positivity into your life, but there are times when we might have some negativity in our lives that come from sources that are beyond our control. How do we deal with them?

Protecting

As much as we witches are supposed to only use our magick for good, there are some out there who have gone rogue from these teachings and sometimes will decide to either attack or summon forces that attack others.

This is an unfortunate truth that makes understanding how to be magickally protected vital. There are many ways to protect yourself: crystals, herbs, or in the case of the following formula, oils.

Protection Oil Recipe

Protection oil is meant to be anointed to keep you safe from magickal or psychic attacks, but you don't have to just use it on yourself. This formula is safe enough that you can use it around your home and property, your car, and even on people who you wish to protect.

You Need

- Carrier Oil (refer to the Wealth Attraction Oil recipe for options)
- The following essential oils: Hyssop, Lavender, Mugwort, and Patchouli

INSTRUCTIONS

1. Use one-eighth of a cup of carrier oil

2. Add the following amounts of essential oils: four drops of Patchouli, three drops of Lavender, one drop of Mugwort, and one drop of Hyssop.

3. As you blend the oils, picture your intentions and smell the aroma, and know that this oil is sacred and magickal.

4. Once blended, label, date it, and store it in a cool, dark place.

5. When using it, only a few drops are necessary. You can put it in your bathwater or directly anoint your third eye chakra as this is connected to your psychic abilities. If you don't wish to anoint yourself then you can sprinkle it on the four cardinal directions around your property, the four corners of your front door, or on the doors of your car.

However, sometimes danger doesn't come from the waking world. This next spell will be helpful in protecting you while you sleep and keeps away negative dreams and entities.

SLEEP PROTECTION SPELL JAR

You Need

- Bay Leaf
- Sea Salt
- Cinnamon
- Sweet Grass
- Sage
- Rosemary
- Rose Buds/Petals
- Spearmint
- Lavender
- Chamomile
- Mullein
- A jar
- One black, light blue, or white candle
- ***Optional:*** A sigil for protection, nightmare prevention, or both

Instructions

1. Wash out and cleanse your jar before you use it; be sure that the jar is well dried.
2. Put enough sea salt in to cover the bottom.
3. Place your herbs inside in layers, the order doesn't matter, only put what is right for you.
4. When the jar is full to the brim, it is good practice to add a sigil. If adding one or more sigils, draw them onto the jar's lid.
5. Close the lid tightly.
6. Use wax from the candle to seal the lid.
7. Put the jar beneath your bed to bring you protection every night as you sleep and keep away negativity as you sleep.
8. Take it out from under your bed to charge and cleanse in the light of the full moon every month before putting it back under your bed.

I hope that in this chapter you have discovered some new ways you can influence your personal life using the universe. In the next chapter we will discuss ways that you can interpret what the universe itself is trying to tell you.

CHAPTER 7

WHAT THE UNIVERSE CAN TELL YOU

Magick isn't just about learning to harness the powers of the universe to help you fulfill your potential, magick is also about learning how to interpret what the universe wants to tell you about yourself and your possible futures.

For thousands of years humans have discovered some wonderfully unique ways to divine their futures, from something as simple as a fire's flames, to something as bizarre as reading different aspects of cheese.

The topic is vast. With that in mind, in this chapter, I will be touching upon three forms of divination: the common astrology and pendulum, and the not so common geomancy.

Astrology

We briefly looked at astrology earlier in the book when determining what type of witch you are. Here we are getting into it a little more. Astrology, in addition to the phases of the moon, can be helpful in determining when you should cast your spell in addition to giving you hints as to your possible destiny.

The zodiac signs that comprise the astrology we are familiar with are associated with Ancient Greece, but in truth astrology goes back as far as the ancient Babylonians and Assyrians.

Astrology can be extremely complicated for beginners, so we will stick with the basics in regards to the zodiacs and their attributes such as the planet, color, etc. associations, as well as magickal properties that have nothing to do with your birth chart.

Before I get down to it, yes Pluto is still considered a planet in regards to astrological readings despite its change in scientific classification.[6]

---

[6] In 2006 the organization which names and decides the status of all celestial bodies (the International Astronomical Union) reclassified, in scientific terms, Pluto as a dwarf planet. However, astrologers still view Pluto to be Scorpio's ruling planet, representing destruction followed by renewal.

The spell types connected to each zodiac refer to the moon and its varying phases, not the sun.

THE ZODIACS

ARIES (MARCH 21—APRIL 20)

- ELEMENT: Fire
- PLANET: Mars
- COLORS: Red
- SPELL TYPES: Anything related to courage, strength, or self-improvement, starting new projects or business ventures. Also good to buy or cleanse any magickal tool that has a blade.

TAURUS (APRIL 21—MAY 20)

- ELEMENT: Earth
- PLANET: Venus
- COLORS: Brown, White
- SPELL TYPES: Anything that concerns the arts, including work that supports new galleries, theaters etc., as well as submitting manuscripts, performing auditions and success of exhibitions and performances. Also anything with the household, security and

stability, and peaceful and cooperative relationships between family members and business partners. Also encourages prosperity and material comfort as well as love spells, but only ones aimed at finding a life partner or strengthening an existing relationship.

Gemini (May 21–June 20)

- ELEMENT: Air
- PLANET: Mercury
- COLORS: Green, turquoise
- SPELL TYPES: A good time for divination and prophecy as well as luck in gambling, communication. Good for working for the positive reception of manuscripts, articles and term papers, increasing web traffic and success in school, including getting into the school of your choice. Also a good time for wishing spells.

Cancer (June 21–July 22)

- ELEMENT: Water
- PLANET: The Moon
- COLORS: Silver, white

- SPELL TYPES: Spells that can calm one's emotional turmoil, to heal any pain or past wrongs within familial relationships, psychic development and divination, protection of the home as well as kitchen and garden witchery. When the moon is waning in Cancer, spells to banish barriers to familial harmony are potent, and when the moon is waxing in Cancer, potent spells are those that increase love and respect within the family.

LEO (JULY 23—AUGUST 22)

- ELEMENT: Fire
- PLANET: The Sun
- COLORS: Gold, orange, yellow
- SPELL TYPES: Any spell related to your animal companions. Encourages good reception for concerts, theater productions and other performances, as well as supporting hobbies. When the moon is waxing in Leo, success in sports as well as spells that increase sex and passion. When the moon is waning in Leo, you can take away barriers that prevent success in sports and move focus away from sex and passion, as well as fighting obsession.

Virgo (August 23–September 22)

- ELEMENT: Earth
- PLANET: Mercury
- COLORS: Dark gray, navy blue, violet
- SPELL TYPES: This is a good time to buy, create, or cleanse any and all tools and altars, as well as cleansing your home; any magick that is related to health and home are also potent at this time, as well as magick related to employment, especially if that employment is related to a health or service career. This is also a good time to do magick that is related to finding good domestic help.

Libra (September 23–October 22)

- ELEMENT: Air
- PLANET: Venus
- COLORS: Green, pale blue
- SPELL TYPES: Any magick that is related to marriage, contractually related partnerships, as well as any and all legal matters and the justice system that includes business contracts, leases, divorces, and criminal court

matters. It is also a good time for spellcasting that makes sure someone gets what's coming to them. When the moon is waxing in Libra, you can cast spells that strengthen marriages and romantic relationships, however when the moon is waning you can weaken those same relationships.

SCORPIO (OCTOBER 23—NOVEMBER 22)

- ELEMENT: Water
- PLANET: Pluto
- COLORS: Blue, burgundy, green
- SPELL TYPES: Spells that are related to fertility, lust, passion, sex, as well as death, rebirth, and inheritance are amplified during this time. When the moon is waxing, it is a good time for spells that increase courage and are for transformation. When the moon is waning, it is a good time for spells that banish negativity and provide protection and self-defense.

SAGITTARIUS (NOVEMBER 23-DECEMBER 21)

- ELEMENT: Fire
- PLANET: Jupiter
- COLORS: Blue, orange
- SPELL TYPES: This is a good time for spells that promote your studies such as getting into a college of your choice, or making a good impression on your teachers. This is also a good time for any type of religious activity like divination or connecting to a higher purpose or gods. You can also implement any plans for long distance travel.

CAPRICORN (DECEMBER 22—JANUARY 19)

- ELEMENT: Earth
- PLANET: Saturn
- COLORS: Black, indigo
- SPELL TYPES: The moon in Capricorn supports any spell that helps with career and business ventures as well as "moving up the ladder," any success in these relations. Also any spells that relate to male fertility, fatherhood, or even your own relationship with

your father. In addition, during a waning moon, any type of banishment is supported.

Aquarius (January 20—February 19)

- ELEMENT: Air
- PLANET: Uranus
- COLORS: Gray, turquoise
- SPELL TYPES: It is not recommended that you perform spells that mostly benefit yourself, instead, this is a great time to focus on any kind of groups or organizations that you belong to that you wish to support. You can also cast spells that benefit friendships and group ties. You can also use this time to reveal or uncover secrets or mysteries that try to stay hidden.

Pisces (February 20—March 20)

- ELEMENT: Water
- PLANET: Neptune
- COLORS: Blue, sea green
- SPELL TYPES: This is a good time for all astral and dream related magick and journeys that expand your consciousness; including all psychic work and divination. This is also a

supportive time for personal development and expanding your boundaries.

It is important to take into consideration both the zodiac and the current phase of the moon. There is further influence on a good spell casting time by the planets themselves, which do include the sun and moon, as detailed below:

THE PLANETS

THE SUN

- SIGN: Leo
- COLORS: Gold and yellow
- GEMSTONE: Ruby
- DAY OF THE WEEK: Sunday
- SPELL TYPES: Abundance, clarity, commonality, confidence, growth, harmony, partnerships, prosperity, truth, wealth

THE MOON

- SIGN: Cancer
- COLOR: Silver
- GEMSTONES: Moonstone, pearl
- DAY OF THE WEEK: Monday

- SPELL TYPES: Cycles, divination, divine feminine, dreams and dreamwork, emotions, finding a path, hidden intentions, secrets, the subconscious, your feminine side

MERCURY

- SIGNS: Gemini, Virgo
- COLOR: Yellow
- GEMSTONES: Citrine, topaz
- DAY OF THE WEEK: Wednesday
- SPELL TYPES: Business, commerce, communication, information, merchants, networking, prosperity, trade, travel, wealth

VENUS

- SIGNS: Taurus, Libra
- COLOR: Green
- GEMSTONES: Emerald, sapphire
- DAY OF THE WEEK: Friday
- SPELL TYPES: Creation of art, garden magick, fertility, harmony, healing, immortality, love, performances, pleasure, relationships, sex

Mars

- SIGN: Aries
- COLOR: Red
- GEMSTONES: Garnet, ruby
- DAY OF THE WEEK: Tuesday
- SPELL TYPES: Breaking love spells, courage, defense, energizing, increasing physical strength, lust, passion

Jupiter

- SIGN: Sagittarius
- COLORS: Deep purple, indigo
- GEMSTONES: Lapis lazuli, sodalite, turquoise
- DAY OF THE WEEK: Thursday
- SPELL TYPES: Authority, fatherhood, legal matters, politics, power, religion

Saturn

- SIGN: Capricorn
- COLORS: Black, gray
- GEMSTONE: Hematite
- DAY OF THE WEEK: Saturday

- **SPELL TYPES:** Boundaries, inevitability, law, leadership, order, responsibility

URANUS

- **SIGN:** Aquarius
- **COLOR:** Aquamarine
- **GEMSTONES:** Clear quartz, labradorite
- **SPELL TYPES:** Creation, discovery, humanitarian ideals, ideas, individuality, industry, invention, progressive ideals, revolution, societies

NEPTUNE

- **SIGN:** Pisces
- **COLORS:** Lilac, violet
- **GEMSTONES:** Amethyst, celestite, fluorite
- **SPELL TYPES:** Divination, glamor, idealism, illusion, imagination, intuition, mysteries, water

PLUTO

- **SIGN:** Scorpio
- **COLORS:** Black, deep red
- **GEMSTONES:** Bloodstone, garnet

- **SPELL TYPES:** Destruction, detection, renewal, research, revealing, uncovering

The zodiac is versatile in how we can use them to power our magick, whether it is the colors, the day of the week, or even the gemstones used. From the sky to the earth, we now move onto pendulum magick.

Pendulums

Pendulums are small weights that are suspended from a piece of chain, cord, or thread. While pendulums are widely available online or in a New Age shop, you can make a pendulum yourself out of anything, whether it is a button or even a paperclip, there isn't a difference in magickal quality whether a pendulum is made or purchased.

The right pendulum for you is one that is comfortable to hold and use, as well as being attractive looking. You can actually get a variety of shapes and sizes if you choose to purchase one, including crystal ones. When it comes to those, quartz crystals are considered a great choice because of the magickal energies they provide, and because crystals are great for healing work. Some of the commercially made pendulums even have a hollow compartment inside them called "sample pendulums" as they are used to find certain things when dowsing, like water, gold, or even oil, you just need to place a small sample of what you are looking for in the compartment.

If you do choose to make one yourself, you first need to take the time and carefully choose your materials, such as natural materials like crystals. If you are thinking about using a metal for the weight, you need to be careful as metal can influence your readings. You also need to avoid conducting materials like glass, plastic, and wood. Your weight should also weigh no more than three ounces. The best shapes are ones that are cylindrical, round, and spherical.

When you are picking something to suspend the weight from, the most commonly used pieces are cords, jewelry chains, string, and thread made from cotton or silk. When choosing your suspension, it is important that the weight hangs freely and that it doesn't interfere with the pendulum's movement. You might also want to buy or make a small bag to carry the pendulum around in and protect it from negative energies.

Using a pendulum is one of, if not the easiest, way to divine information, however that comes with lots of practice, which starts by learning on your own, as having other people around could be distracting. You can operate your pendulum with either your dominant or non-dominant hand.

Rest your elbow on a table if you're sitting down and hold your pendulums' suspension between your thumb and first finger without a lot of pressure. You also need to keep your arms and legs uncrossed as crossing them will close yourself off from the pendulum and it will not work for you properly.

Gently let the pendulum swing in different directions to get used to the feeling. You can experiment by holding the suspension at different lengths to see if it responds easier for you in a certain position; once you're comfortable with the movement, use your free hand to stop it. Once it's still, that's when you'll start to learn its movements when it is answering your questions. First ask which movement is a 'yes' response; it doesn't matter if you ask aloud or in your head. You may not succeed in learning the first time, you just need to keep practicing.

Once you have received your 'yes' answer, you then ask the movements for three other answers; 'no,' 'I don't know,' and 'I don't want to answer.' If you don't use your pendulum after a significant amount of time, then you will have to become familiar with the responses again by asking the same questions as the movements might change.

After you've become comfortable with the specific movements, start asking questions that you know the answer to, such as confirming the date of your birthday. You can deliberately ask wrong questions to test it further. When you are comfortable, you can start asking questions you would like the answer to, but you need to be careful when using a pendulum as you could accidentally have your own will influence the outcome of the reading and it may turn out to be incorrect, the same is said for wishful thinking.

And never forget that a pendulum is not a toy! Never ask a pendulum flippant questions as you will receive flippant answers in return.

There are few limits to the types of questions you can ask, like ones about your future. There is no right or wrong time to use it.

While pendulums are utilized above the ground, this final category of divination can be used on the ground.

Geomancy

If you are a beginner, then the word geomancy may be new to you. To be honest, even at an intermediate level, you may not have encountered it as of yet. If that's the case, I am here to give you a basic tutelage about this form of divination.

Geomancy is the art of divination that traditionally uses marks made on the earth and are interpreted from there. There are many in existence, but I will be taking you through one of the more popular methods in this book. It uses 16 geomantic figures that are created using a random series of marks. This particular method is easy to do, but might be a little difficult in regards to interpretation.

In this method, you begin your casting by focusing on your question such as, "is my job interview going to go well?" Once it's stuck inside your head, you start making a geomantic figure. You do this by creating a series of four rows of vertical lines on the ground from right to left. You may also choose to use a piece of paper.

Then you count out the number of marks in each row to determine the dot(s) needed to fully create the figure. If there is an odd number of marks *(like 1, 5, 17, etc.)* then you use only one dot for the figure. You use two dots for the figure if the number of marks is even *(like 2, 6, 18, etc.)*. Each part of the figure is named, there's the **head**, the **neck**, the **body**, and the **feet**. Each figure has a different combination of dots. Here's a brief example of a figure with two of each dot combination:

1 dot *(odd number of marks)*

2 dots *(even number of marks)*

1 dot *(odd number of marks)*

2 dots *(even number of marks)*

This resulting figure is known as "Amissio, the loss." Each figure has a different title; but not only that, each figure has a different association with elements, zodiac signs, planets, months, and even days of the week. We will very briefly go over each figure, where I name each figure and their mark numbers in the order of head to feet as well as the associations listed.

PUER—THE BOY (1,1,2,1)

ELEMENT: Fire

ZODIAC: Aries

PLANET: Mars

MONTH: March

DAY: Monday

AMISSIO—THE LOSS (1,2,1,2)

ELEMENT: Earth

ZODIAC: Taurus

PLANET: Venus

MONTH: September

DAY: Friday

ALBUS—THE WHITE (2,2,1,2)

ELEMENT: Air

ZODIAC: Gemini

PLANET: Mercury

MONTH: June

DAY: Wednesday

POPULUS—THE PEOPLE (2,2,2,2)

ELEMENT: Water

ZODIAC: Cancer

PLANET: Moon

MONTH: December

DAY: Monday

FORTUNA MAJOR— MAJOR FORTUNE (2,2,1,1)

ELEMENT: Fire

ZODIAC: Leo

PLANET: Sun

MONTH: January

DAY: Sunday

CONJUNCTIO— THE UNION (2,1,1,2)

ELEMENT: Earth

ZODIAC: Virgo

PLANET: Mercury

MONTH: August

DAY: Wednesday

PUELLA—THE GIRL (1,2,1,1)

ELEMENT: Air

ZODIAC: Libra

PLANET: Venus

MONTH: September

DAY: Wednesday

RUBEUS—THE RED (2,1,2,2)

ELEMENT: Water

ZODIAC: Scorpio

PLANET: Mars

MONTH: March

DAY: Tuesday

ACQUISITIO—GAIN (2,1,2,1)

ELEMENT: Fire

ZODIAC: Sagittarius

PLANET: Jupiter

MONTH: March

DAY: Thursday

CARCER—THE PRISON (1,2,2,1)

ELEMENT: Earth

ZODIAC: Capricorn

PLANET: Saturn

MONTH: February

DAY: Saturday

TRISTITIA—THE SADNESS (2,2,2,1)

ELEMENT: Air

ZODIAC: Aquarius

PLANET: Saturn

MONTH: October

DAY: Saturday

LAETITIA—THE JOY (1,2,2,2)

ELEMENT: Water

ZODIAC: Pisces

PLANET: Jupiter

MONTH: April

DAY: Thursday

CAUDA DRACONIS—
THE DRAGON'S TAIL (1,1,1,2)

ELEMENT: Fire

ZODIAC: Sagittarius

PLANET: South Node of the Moon

MONTH: November

DAY: Saturday

CAPUT DRACONIS—
THE DRAGON'S HEAD (2,1,1,1)

ELEMENT: Earth

ZODIAC: Virgo

PLANETS: Venus and Jupiter

MONTH: August

DAY: Saturday

FORTUNA MINOR— THE MINOR FORTUNE (1,1,2,2)

ELEMENT: Fire

ZODIAC: Leo

PLANET: Sun

MONTH: April

DAY: Sunday

VIA—THE WAY (1,1,1,1)

ELEMENT: Water

ZODIAC: Cancer

PLANET: Moon

MONTH: July

DAY: Monday

So, it appears that we have a form of divination that has a connection to astrology, albeit a minor one. As for divining the figures, each one can either be positive or negative, or even both depending on the question being asked. A simple divination would use a single figure but there is a more complex way that we will not be discussing, but if you are interested in using Geomancy in your life, then feel free to check it out on your own. This is a divination that I highly recommend!

I would like to remind you that this is only a small sample of what you can do when it comes to learning Geomancy, the earth is a vast resource for us, whether it is food, or telling our fortunes.

CONCLUSION

And now my friends, the time has come for our paths to diverge for a while. I hope that you have had as wonderful a time with me as I have with you.

Throughout our journey together you have learned the basics of how to keep your space sacred, your energy in top shape, and how to keep your energy well from overflowing.

But you have also learned much more than that, you have learned just how vast our craft can actually be, that there is no singular road to take when we practice our magick, from communing with the earth herself, to exploring the universe, and even other dimensions.

You have also learned how to harness bounty from the world to perform a variety of spells that will benefit you in such positive ways. From something as tricky as finding love, to something as simple as getting a good night's sleep!

You have also learned to use both the earth and the heavens to help chart your life paths, and to possibly answer some important questions about your future.

Remember to always focus on what's positive and good. Life is always going to throw things at you, ranging from small annoyances to extreme challenges.

If you keep up that positive spirit, you'll find that practically anything is possible, whether that is performing tasks that are mundane or magickal.

I WISH YOU ALL A BLESSED MAGICKAL JOURNEY
GOING FORWARD

THANK YOU FOR READING

I just wanted to say thank you for purchasing my book. There are so many books out there but you decided to take the time to read through mine, and for that I am so truly grateful.

Before we finish our journey together, **could you do me a small favor and leave a quick review? Posting a review is the best way to support an independent author's work and it would mean so much to me to hear from you.**

To leave a review please scan a QR Code below:

Leave a review: Amazon US   Leave a review: Amazon UK

Thank you and have a magickal day!

Yours gratefully,

Eleanor Clemm

P.S. If you enjoyed this book, download your FREE gift "50 Powerful Spell Jar Recipes" by heading over to:
Http://FireBoltBooks.com

REFERENCES

Backlund, R. (2018, May 10). *Here's How To Write A Spell That Manifests *Exactly* What You Want Out Of Life.* Elite Daily. https://www.elitedaily.com/lifestyle/how-to-write-a-spell-to-manifest-what-you-want

Cassandra. (2016, September 12). *A Simple, but Powerful Manifestation Spell.* The Sacred Middle. https://www.thesacredmiddle.com/blog/a-simple-but-powerful-manifestation-spell

Chamberlain, L. (2020a). *Wicca Book of Spells : A Beginner's Book of Shadows for Wiccans, Witches, & Other Practitioners of Magick.* Wicca Shorts.

Chamberlain, L. (2020b). *WICCA FOR BEGINNERS : a Guide to Wiccan Beliefs, Rituals, Magick, and Witchcraft.* Sterling Ethos.

Chauran, A. (2017). *Runes for Beginners : Simple Divination and Interpretation*. Llewellyn Worldwide, Ltd.

Cherry, K. (2015, February 2). *9 Common Dreams and What They Supposedly Mean*. Verywell Mind; Verywellmind. https://www.verywellmind.com/understanding-your-dreams-2795935

The Cut. (2020, April 27). *A Beginner's Guide to Tarot Cards*. The Cut. https://www.thecut.com/article/tarot-cards.html

Dream interpretation. (2022, February 3). Wikipedia. https://en.m.wikipedia.org/wiki/Dream_interpretation

Dugan, E. (2008). *Herb Magick for Beginners : Down-to-Earth Enchantments*. Llewellyn Publications.

5 Clear Signs the Spell You Cast is Working. (2019, March 12). Spells8. https://spells8.com/lessons/signs-spell-working/

Frazier, K. (2017). *Crystals for beginners : The Guide to Get Started With the Healing Power of Crystals*. Althea Press.

Greenleaf, C. (2020). *The Witch's Guide to Ritual : Spells, Incantations, and Inspired Ideas for an Enchanted Life.* Mango Publishing.

Hart, A. (n.d.-a). *How Glamor Magick Works & 3 Glamor Spells To Try Today.* The Traveling Witch. Retrieved April 26, 2022, from https://thetravelingwitch.com/blog/how-glamor-magick-works-3-glamor-spells-to-try-today

Hart, A. (n.d.-b). *How To Cleanse: The Ultimate Guide For New Witches.* The Traveling Witch. Retrieved April 20, 2022, from https://thetravelingwitch.com/blog/2017/11/21/how-to-cleanse-the-ultimate-guide-for-new-witches

Holland, K. (2018, December 3). *Are Auras Real? 15 FAQs About Color, Meaning, More.* Healthline. https://www.healthline.com/health/what-is-an-aura

Jones, K. C., & Kawamura, F. (2014). *Fortune-telling book of colors.* Chronicle Books.

Lindberg, S. (2020, August 24). *What are chakras? Meaning, location, and how to unblock them.* Healthline. https://www.healthline.com/health/what-are-chakras

Moules, J. (2019, April 15). *Align Your Chakras With These 7 Chakra Yoga Poses.* YogiApproved™. https://www.yogiapproved.com/chakra-yoga-chakra-alignment/

Peterson, E. (2022a, February 23). *How to Prepare for a Ritual or Spell.* I Love Spells. https://www.ilovespells.com/how-to-prepare-for-a-ritual-or-spell/

Peterson, E. (2022b, February 23). *Spell Timing - When is the Best Time to Cast Magick Spells?* I Love Spells. https://www.ilovespells.com/best-time-for-casting-a-spell/#Spell_Timing_and_Choosing_the_Best_Phase_of_the_Moon

Pond, D. (2020). *Astrology for Beginners : Learn to Read Your Birth Chart.* Llewellyn.

Robbins, S., & Greenaway, L. (2014). Wiccapedia : A Modern-Day White Witch's Guide. Sterling Ethos.

Sabin, T. (2006). *Wicca for beginners : Fundamentals of Philosophy & Practice.* Llewellyn Publications.

Sheetal. (2020, April 27). *5 WAYS TO USE INTENTION OILS ATTRACT MONEY, LOVE, PROTECTION & MORE.* YouTube https://www.youtube.com/watch?v=I5rdX2ei TZY

Stelter, G. (2016, October 4). *A Beginner's Guide to the 7 Chakras and Their Meanings*. Healthline; Healthline Media. https://www.healthline.com/health/fitness-exercise/7-chakras

Stewart, T. (2016, August 10). *5 Steps to Figure Out What Kind of Witch You Are*. The Witch of Lupine Hollow. https://witchoflupinehollow.com/2016/08/10/5-steps-to-figure-out-what-kind-of-witch-you-are/

Stewart, T. (2018, March 5). *How to Use Astrology to Figure Out What Kind of Witch You Are*. The Witch of Lupine Hollow. https://witchoflupinehollow.com/2018/03/05/use-astrology-figure-kind-witch/

Stokes, V. (2021, May 6). *How to Open Your Third Eye Chakra for Spiritual Awakening*. Healthline. https://www.healthline.com/health/mind-body/how-to-open-your-third-eye

Teaandrosemary2. (2020, November 2). *3 Easy Glamour Spells For Enhanced Beauty Using Witchcraft*. Tea & Rosemary. https://teaandrosemary.com/3-easy-glamour-spells-for-enhanced-beauty-using-witchcraft/

themanicnami. (2017, April 17). *Sleep Protection Spell Jar*. Witchy Things. https://themanicnami.tumblr.com/post/159693967406/sleep-protection-spell-jar

Vondechii's Vault. (2020, August 15). *Different Types of Witches*. YouTube. https://www.youtube.com/watch?v=JEDNhA1G43E&list=LL&index=5

Webster, R. (2002). *Pendulum Magick for Beginners: Tap into Your Inner Wisdom*. Llewellyn Publications.

Webster, R. (2004). *Candle Magick For Beginners : The Simplest Magick You Can Do*. Llewellyn Publications.

Webster, R. (2011). *Geomancy for Beginners: Simple Techniques for Earth Divination*. Llewellyn Publications.

Webster, R. (2017). *Amulets & Talismans For Beginners : How to Choose, Make & Use Magickal Objects*. Woodbury, Minnesota Llewellyn Publications.

Webster, R. (2021). *Color Magick for Beginners: Use the Power of Color to Attract Luck, Health & Harmony* (First Edition, Thirteenth Printing).

Llewellyn Publications. (Original work published 2006)

Wigington, P. (2019, May 9). *Magickal Banishing Spells and Folklore.* Learn Religions. https://www.learnreligions.com/about-magickal-banishing-2562757

Wigington, P. (2019, May 24). *How to Get Rid of Unwanted Spirits.* Learn Religions. https://www.learnreligions.com/getting-rid-of-unwanted-spirits-2561750

Wigington, P. (2019, June 25). *How to Magickally Ground, Center, and Shield.* Learn Religions. https://www.learnreligions.com/grounding-centering-and-shielding-4122187

Wigington, P. (2019, June 25). *Simple Spellwork for Protection Magick.* Learn Religions. https://www.learnreligions.com/magick-protection-spells-and-rituals-2562176

Wikipedia. (2022, January 14). *Coven.* Wikipedia. https://en.m.wikipedia.org/wiki/Coven

Witchcraft Symbols - Symbols To Enhance Your Magick | Well Divined. (2021, August 31). Well Divined. https://welldivined.com/witchcraft/witchcraft-symbols/

The witches' cookery. (2021, March 5). *How to know what Witch you are | 20 Types of Witches*. YouTube. https://www.youtube.com/watch?v=r_7riS3UVUY&list=PLjaMlOACREVcyDa_uk5iSOT_9A3HxAXuB&index=2

The Witchipedian. (2009, October 5). *Pluto*. The Witchipedia. https://witchipedia.com/astrology/pluto/

The Witchipedian. (2016a, June 3). *Jupiter*. The Witchipedia. https://witchipedia.com/astrology/mars/

The Witchipedian. (2016b, June 3). *Mars*. The Witchipedia. https://witchipedia.com/astrology/mars/

The Witchipedian. (2019a, July 9). *Venus*. The Witchipedia. https://witchipedia.com/astrology/venus/

The Witchipedian. (2019b, August 3). *Jupiter*. The Witchipedia. https://witchipedia.com/astrology/jupiter/

The Witchipedian. (2019c, August 3). *Mercury*. The Witchipedia. https://witchipedia.com/astrology/mercury/

The Witchipedian. (2019d, September 1). *Saturn*. The Witchipedia. https://witchipedia.com/astrology/saturn/

The Witchipedian. (2019e, September 2). *Moon*. The Witchipedia. https://witchipedia.com/astrology/moon/

The Witchipedian. (2019f, September 2). *Neptune*. The Witchipedia. https://witchipedia.com/astrology/neptune/

The Witchipedian. (2019g, October 5). *Sun*. The Witchipedia. https://witchipedia.com/astrology/sun/

The Witchipedian. (2019h, October 5). *Uranus*. The Witchipedia. https://witchipedia.com/astrology/uranus/

The Witchipedian. (2019i, November 17). *Spell Timing*. The Witchipedia. https://witchipedia.com/how-to/spell-timing/

You are a Lunar Witch. (n.d.). The Witch of Lupine Hollow. https://lupinehollow.kartra.com/page/lunar-witch

You are a Solar Witch. (n.d.). The Witch of Lupine Hollow. https://lupinehollow.kartra.com/page/solar-witch

You are a Wild Witch. (n.d.). The Witch of Lupine Hollow.

https://lupinehollow.kartra.com/page/wild-witch

You are an Astro Witch. (n.d.). The Witch of Lupine Hollow.
https://lupinehollow.kartra.com/page/astro-witch

You are an Empath Witch. (n.d.). The Witch of Lupine Hollow.
https://lupinehollow.kartra.com/page/empath-witch

You are an Warrior Witch. (n.d.). The Witch of Lupine Hollow.
https://lupinehollow.kartra.com/page/warrior-witch

You're a Shadow Witch! (n.d.). The Witch of Lupine Hollow.
https://witchoflupinehollow.com/quiz-result-shadow-witch/

FireBoltBooks.com

Printed in Great Britain
by Amazon